P9-EEG-114

Derek C. Hutchinson's Guide to

SEA KAYAKING

Second Edition

Derek C. Hutchinson

The Globe Pequot Press • Old Saybrook, Connecticut

© 1985, 1990 by Derek C. Hutchinson.

All rights reserved. No part of this book may be reproduced without permission from the publisher, except by a reviewer who may quote brief passages in a review; nor may any part of this book be reproduced, stored in a retrieval system or transmitted in any form or by any means, electronic, mechanical, photocopying, recording or other, without permission from the publisher. Requests for permission should be made in writing to The Globe Pequot Press, P.O. Box 833, Old Saybrook, Connecticut 06475.

*T*his book is dedicated to Alistair Wilson, Tom Caskey, Chris Jowsey, and George Peck—true friends and my companions in search of the killer whale of Prince William Sound, Alaska. And to all those who have chosen to venture upon the sea in the most beautiful of all solo craft—the Hunter's Boat or kayak of the Arctic.

Photo on Contents page by Jim Appleby
Photo on Acknowledgments page by Chris Jowsey

Technical illustrations are by the author.
Illustrations on pages 6, 19, 28, 40, 50, 102,
    and 120 are from Fridtjof Nansen, *The First Crossing of Greenland* (London, 1892). Title page illustration from Captain Koldewey, *The German Arctic Expedition of 1869–1874* (London, 1874).
Chapter headings illustration from Leslie, Jameson, and Murray, *Narrative of Discovery and Adventure in the Polar Seas and Regions* (Edinburgh & London, 1830).

Library of Congress Cataloging-in-Publication Data

Hutchinson, Derek C.
    [Guide to sea kayaking]
    Derek C. Hutchinson's Guide to sea kayaking / Derek C. Hutchinson.
    — 2nd ed.
        p.   cm.
    ISBN 0-87106-473-1
    1. Sea kayaking.   I. Title.   II. Title: Guide to sea kayaking.
    GV788.5.H87   1990   89-71368
    797.1'22—dc20   CIP

Manufactured in the United States of America
Second Edition/Third Printing

CONTENTS

ACKNOWLEDGMENTS

I am fortunate to number among my friends those whom I would consider to be the best in the world of the men and women who paddle the kayak on the open sea. It has been through their stories and my own experiences that I have been able to write this book. My thanks to Frank Goodman for his invaluable help, especially on the subject of plastic sea kayaks, and to Chris Jowsey, Martin Meling, Alan Byde, and Clive Hutchinson. I am also indebted to Larry Willis of Florida for his alligator noises. To Molly Jones, mother of the late Dr. Mike Jones. To Mike Clark of *Canoeing* magazine; Derek Bamforth of Pacific Canoe Base, Victoria, British Columbia; Gary and Mercia Sixta of the Vancouver Kayak Club; Will Nordby of San Francisco; Matt Broze of the Washington Kayak Club; Steve Sinclair of Force 10, Elk, California; Werner Furrer, kayak designer of Washington State, Robert Licht of Sea Trek Ocean Kayaking Center, Sausalito, California, and Gary Birnham of Sydney, Australia.

A big thank you must go to Mary Padwick, who suffered the job of correcting, organizing, and typing my scrambled manuscript and to Ron Leamon, who undertook the job of editing the whole affair. Thanks also to Dave (Dancingbear) Hunsaker of Juneau, Alaska, for making me see the need for this book.

I am also grateful for the facilities offered by the Literary and Philosophical Society of Newcastle-upon-Tyne.

And thank you to the thief who ransacked my car and stole my briefcase, but left the separate sheets of this manuscript spread around among the trees of a nearby park—in the rain.

INTRODUCTION

I stood on a green velvet lawn and held the kayak paddle tightly in my clenched hands. It was the spring of 1963, and suitably spaced around me were about ten other individuals all clutching their paddles tightly. We faced in the same direction, and the object of our attention was an older, rather rounded gentleman who also held a paddle. He had demonstrated the correct method of holding and handling this strange piece of equipment. We in turn tried to copy his movements. Paddles flailed through the air and every now and again there would be a loud clack as paddle collided with paddle. I decided that I was completely uncoordinated but at least I felt some comfort when I looked at what appeared to be a host of ruptured windmills.

It was a beautiful Saturday morning, however, and the sun was shining. My Education Authority had already held a number of "taster" courses in outdoor education for teachers in their service. A few of us at the school where I taught felt that the potential entertainment value of these courses was too good to be ignored, so we had given them our wholehearted support. The "Introduction to Camping" weekend had been fun, but as far as the "Introduction to Rock Climbing" was concerned, I had decided that discretion was the better part of valor. I am terrified of heights and I felt that the sight of a grown man crying might have upset the weekend for everyone else. I had decided to save myself for the kayaking weekend on the grounds that I liked water and that if I capsized, I would not have far to fall.

Around us on the lawn lay kayaks of varying shapes and sizes. I still felt demoralized by my apparent lack of coordination, and I was relieved when we were asked to follow our instructor over to a small outdoor swimming pool. This worthy man got into one of the kayaks with an ease that amazed me and proceeded to demonstrate the forward paddling stroke on the water. He showed us how to stop the boat and also how to paddle backward. To finish off, he pointed out to the onlookers that it was vital that everyone should be able to vacate the kayak easily in the event of a capsize. He demonstrated this to his now rather nervous audience by suddenly turning his boat upside down, waiting for about three seconds, then exiting from the cockpit. I was horrified, but he surfaced unhurriedly, with a beaming face. Now it was our turn, he announced, and suddenly I felt ill.

One by one my associates capsized beneath the clear blue water, and more and more I wished that I had not come on what had turned out to be a masochistic if not suicidal weekend. Then it was my turn. It was obvious to any fool that the cockpit was far too small and that I would stick fast. I did not relish the thought of a claustrophobic, choking death at the hands of this madman—and said so. We talked, he persuaded, and I capsized. Suddenly I was standing up to my waist in water, and miraculously I had survived. I don't even remember leaving the cockpit and yet it had worried me sick. I decided there was nothing to it and I was all attention when our instructor announced that he was going to give us a demonstration of handling techniques that would be something for us to aim for.

I don't know what I expected to see, but as before, he entered the kayak with an easy familiarity. He pulled a spray cover over the cockpit coaming and it was as if he had, by some freak of evolution, suddenly grown a kayak where his legs should have been. The boat became an extension of his body.

To say that it was a delight to watch this man move his kayak around in this tiny pool would be an understatement. He handled and held his paddle as gently as some fairy queen would hold her wand, and the ballet he performed with that boat would have done credit to Swan Lake. Every movement was controlled, every lean was the picture of grace. On the face of this artist—and he was an artist—was a look of utter contentment. A glance around the faces of the other onlookers told me that they were also enthralled. I had arrived on this course rather bored and indifferent, but this man had held me spellbound. His name was Alan Byde and he was a senior coach with the British Canoe Union. This was the highest pinnacle a man could reach and I decided that I wanted to be like him. That first capsize seems a lifetime ago, but the same Alan who is now my friend would be the first to admit that my life has never been quite the same since.

Ocean kayaking is a sport in which age and sex are not barriers, and I cannot think of many physical activities that can be done equally well by men and women between the ages of twenty and sixty all in the same group. Paddling a kayak is also a very personal thing. Once secure inside the cockpit and snug on the molded bucket seat, it soon becomes obvious to the occupant that it is a boat that is worn rather than sat in. Every mood and movement of the sea is transmitted through the hull of the kayak to the paddler's nervous system. In this way a union is built up between the man and the sea.

The challenge of the ocean kayak is more than a physical one, and I've especially found the navigational aspects of the sport mentally stimulating. Because of the boat's obvious restrictions, any navigation has to go back to basics. Because the paddler can have no sextant to locate his position or log to gauge his speed, he has to rely solely on his compass, a chart, and a good memory. I remember as if it were yesterday the days of waiting prior to my second attempt to make a crossing of the North Sea. Every evening we would get out the chart and plan the long trip anticipating good weather for the following day. With nervous apprehension, we finally set off at 6:30 A.M. on a morning early in June. We knew that the fast tidal streams change direction every six hours and that the mainlands of England and Belgium in the area of our crossing were below sea level. This would mean that we would have no land upon which to fix our eyes. Thirty-one hours later, to our relief and satisfaction, we landed exactly where we had intended—on the beach at Ostend.

Even the shortest journeys by kayak are true voyages of discovery. It may be along a familiar bit of tree-lined coast or in and out of the jetties and moorings of some seaport town or city. Wherever it may be, you will see the world, your companions, and yourself from a completely different angle; and if you are like me, it will be an experience that never becomes jaded. For those who are unable to travel far from their homes, the same piece of water can be paddled over many times—the backdrop may remain the same, but the stage is always different.

I have written this book so that it is not simply a book on how to kayak. Rather, it is a book on how to kayak in such a way as to live to kayak another day. In it I have attempted to provide enough information to stimulate the experienced paddler and to help those who are becoming proficient to overcome many of the problems and situations they may be faced with. I have assumed a certain level of expertise on the part of the reader and have not described all the basic techniques and maneuvers.

Most of your kayaking may be done as part of coastal touring or as island-hopping trips in areas familiar to you. Once in a while, however, you may be driven by a mixture of curiosity and a sense of adventure to transport your seaworthy little boat to wild, faraway, and unfamiliar coastlines. There you will find that just about anything can happen and usually does. That is why this book is filled with facts that may not solve the problem, but at least insure that the problem itself will not come as a great surprise.

To add a little spice to the text, I have included a number of old prints and descriptions of kayaks and kayaking written by early explorers of the Arctic and North America. Because I am a romantic at heart, I find these prints and historical accounts both interesting and inspirational. I hope you will likewise enjoy them and will find your thoughts turning to them again and again—especially on long crossings.

*   *   *

No sport stands still, and the world of sea kayaking is no exception. I have tried to find the time between my own paddling adventures to update this little volume. Since the book was first published, a number of problems have come to notice. I had been going to say "new" problems, but of course the problems are as old as the hills. It is just that the kayak has given us the opportunity to face them firsthand.

While paddling along one of Florida's dreamy, quiet waterways, I surprised an alligator. Did I say *I* surprised the alligator? Believe that if you will! The creature took off from the small hidden beach at high speed. It must have been at least eighteen feet long—well, all right, perhaps it *was* only eight feet long, but then the sun was in my eyes! That alligator is now much wiser. It now knows, for instance, that human beings can change color from pink to white in a matter of seconds without the use of dyes or bleaches. Later the same year, a tick strolled along my foredeck and attempted to savage me. Fear of Lyme disease gave me the strength to fight it off with my paddle, and I realized it was just something else for the global kayaker to think about.

Apart from the problems posed by deer ticks and alligators, I felt the need to mention the danger of shark attack. The chapter dealing with waves has also been expanded, and a movement diagram for the screw roll should make it easier for those who wish to teach themselves this technique. Finally, I decided that plastic sea kayaks also deserved a place in the new edition.

The Globe Pequot Press assumes no liability for accidents happening to, or injuries sustained by, readers who engage in the activities described in this book.

THE KAYAK

The Beginnings

It was the Eskimo's kayak that started it all, of course. But the early explorers who gazed upon this strange little boat of driftwood and skin probably never dreamed it would later be adapted and used for recreational purposes and on the oceans of the world. Those early explorers were impressed—even awed— by the kayak and the skills displayed by the original kayakers, and today's paddlers can find instruction as well as entertainment in the writings of Fridtjof Nansen, David Crantz, and others. In Nansen's detailed description, one is struck by the Eskimo's ingenuity in utilizing available materials:

It has an internal framework of wood. This, of which the reader can, I hope, form some conception from the accompanying drawing, was formerly always made of driftwood, usually of the white wood, which is the lightest [fig. 1]. For the ribs, osiers were sometimes used, from willow bushes which are found growing far up the fiords. In later days they have got into the habit of buying European boards of spruce and Scotch fir in the west coast colonies, although drift-wood is still considered preferable, especially on account of its lightness.

This framework is covered externally with skins, as a rule with the skin of the saddleback seal (*Phoca groenlandica*), or of the bladder-nose or hood seal (*Cystophora cristata*). The latter is not so durable or so water-tight as the former; but the skin of a young bladder-nose, in which the pores are not yet very large, is considered good enough. . . . the skin of the bearded seal (*Phoca barbata*). . .is reckoned the best and strongest. . . . the skin of the great ringed seal (*Phoca foetida*) is also used. . . .

. . .The preparation of the skins, and the sewing and stretching them on the kaiak, belongs to the women's department; it is not very easy work, and woe to them if the skin sits badly or is too slack. They feel it a great disgrace.

In the middle of the kaiak's deck there is a hole just large enough to enable a man to get his legs through it and to sit down; his thighs almost entirely fill the aperture. Thus it takes a good deal of practice before one can slip into or out of the kaiak with any sort of ease. The hole is surrounded by the kaiak-ring, which consists of a hoop of wood. It stands a little more than an inch (3 or 3½ centimetres) above the kaiak's deck, and the waterproof jacket, as we shall presently see, is drawn over it. At the spot where the rower sits, pieces of old kaiak skin are laid in the bottom over the ribs, with a piece of bearskin or other fur to make the seat softer.

As a rule, each hunter makes his kaiak for himself, and it is fitted to the man's size just like a garment. The bottom of the kaiak is pretty flat, sloping to a very obtuse angle (probably about 140°) in the middle. The kaiak narrows evenly in, both fore and aft, and comes to a point at both ends. It has no keel, but its underpart at both ends is generally provided with bone flanges, for the most part of whale-rib, designed

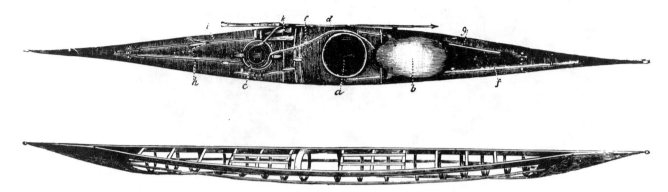

1. Eskimo kayak and frame. Letters on the original illustration indicate placement of hunting weapons. (From Fridtjof Nansen, *Eskimo Life* [London, 1893], p. 44.)

A Greenlander in his kajak is indeed an object of wonder and delight, and his sable sea dress, shining with rows of white bone buttons, gives him a splendid appearance. He rows with extreme celerity in this boat. . . . He dreads no storm: as long as a ship can carry its top-sail, he braves the mountainous billows, darting over them like a bird, and even when completely buried in the waves, he soon re-appears skimming along the surface. If a breaker threatens to overset him, he supports himself in an erect position by his oar, or if he is actually upset, he restores himself to his balance by one swing of his paddle. But if he loses the oar, it is certain death, unless speedy succour be at hand.

Some Europeans have by dint of application attained sufficient command of the kajak for a calm-weather voyage; but they seldom venture to fish in it, and are totally helpless in dangerous situations. The Greenlanders possess in the management of this vessel, a dexterity peculiar to themselves, which excites a fearful interest in the spectator. . . . (David Crantz, History of Greenland: Including an Account of the Mission Carried on by the Bretheren of That Country, *2 vols. [London: Longman, Hurst, Rees, Orme, and Brown, 1820], 1:139–40.)*

to save the skin from being ripped up by drift-ice, or by stones when the kaiak is beached. Both points are commonly provided with knobs of bone, partly for ornament, partly for protection as well.

Across the deck, in front of the kaiak-ring, six thongs are usually fastened, and from three to five behind the rower. Under these thongs weapons and implements are inserted, so that they lie safe and handy for use. (Fridtjof Nansen, *Eskimo Life,* trans. William Archer [London: Longmans, Green, and Co. 1893], pp. 44–45.)

Although Nansen writes as if there were only one design, Eskimo kayak designs varied considerably from place to place (see fig. 2). Differences in design are easy to understand when the kayaks were from areas separated by considerable distance, but designs from the same area often had marked differences as well. These variations—some subtle and some not so subtle—were due to a number of factors. The function of the kayak was a primary consideration in the design. Some were designed to carry heavy loads and consequently had a lot of freeboard. Others were designed to be sleek and fast for hunting. Still others were designed to carry more than one person and were built with long journeys in mind. The type of sea and weather conditions to be faced also influenced design. Kayaks intended for use in sheltered fjords tended to be low in the water with little freeboard. Boats that had to cope with rough seas often had steeply pitched decks.

These uses for the kayak suggest how important the kayak was to the Eskimo. Indeed, it was an almost indispensable part of their way of life. But that way of life has passed now and the skin boats are nearly gone. The Aleuts and Inuits go about their business in dories with outboard motors. I like to think, though, that

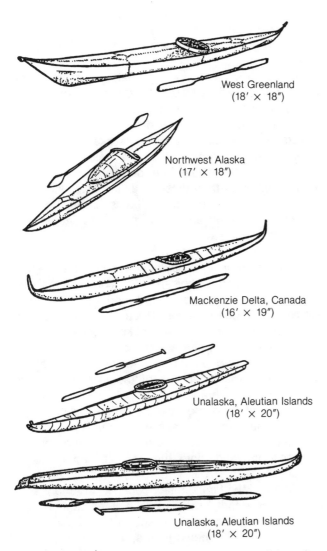

West Greenland
(18′ × 18″)

Northwest Alaska
(17′ × 18″)

Mackenzie Delta, Canada
(16′ × 19″)

Unalaska, Aleutian Islands
(18′ × 20″)

Unalaska, Aleutian Islands
(18′ × 20″)

2. Inuit and Aleut skin boats that have influenced modern sea kayak design.

in modern replicas of the "hunter's boat" we can keep the skills and some of the spirit alive.

The Modern Sea Kayak

Since the latter part of the nineteenth century when John Macgregor brought his heavy Rob Roy canoe to the attention of the public, numerous craft supposedly modeled upon native North American and Arctic boats have been built. Many of these were strange looking indeed, and few resembled even the clumsiest of the original skin boats.

In the early 1960s the advent of fiber glass to the boating scene gave designers a medium in which graceful curves were easier to reproduce. No longer were they restricted by the limitations of lath and fabric. The result was the appearance over the next decade of a number of sea kayaks that were aesthetically pleasing and clearly influenced by the Arctic skin boats. It is only since the beginning of the 1970s that the real potential of the sea kayak has been realized.

At present in Britain there are five or six leading sea kayak designs, and all are based on the styles of the original skin boats of North America and the Arctic. If the reader of these pages detects a preference on my part for these boats, it is because they and a few others being produced in Europe have been proved internationally in a variety of rough water conditions.

In contrast, the use in modern-day North America of the one-person kayak is still in its embryonic stage. (Credit must go to the North Americans for pioneering the use of the two-person or double kayak on the open sea, for making seaworthy double kayaks, and for proving them in a variety of conditions.) During the last few years the popularity of the one-person kayak has increased dramatically in North America, and numerous one-person kayak designs have appeared on the market to keep pace with the demand. Many of these kayaks have been designed to cope with sea conditions that can be found only in certain areas, while others have had no time to be tested and proved in the variety of conditions necessary to give the kayaks universal appeal.

Challenges of Kayak Design. In all fairness it must be said that anyone who designs kayaks for use on the open sea is faced with a number of complex and frustrating problems. To satisfy discerning paddlers, the finished masterpiece must be light enough for anyone to toss onto a vehicle, yet must be strong and heavy enough to withstand the pressures and batterings of rough usage. A kayak must also run straight at all times—even in the most trying conditions—yet turn easily when the need arises. It must be stable enough to give the timid confidence, but narrow enough to make rolling an untroubled maneuver. The hull must be voluminous enough to accommodate a mountain of equipment, but the amount of freeboard must be kept to a minimum. The seat should be comfortable and give good support for many hours, and it must also be in the correct position so that the occupant trims the boat when it is paddled. High seats breed high speeds and instability. Low seats give stability, but as a bonus they can also provide the paddler with bruised and wet elbows and skinned knuckles.

Designers face all these tantalizing dilemmas in a variety of ways with the end result that there is no such thing as a perfect sea kayak. All are a compromise in one way or another, and when making a decision as to which one to buy, a paddler or potential paddler must use his own judgment, tempered by the advice of more experienced friends and as many "dry runs" in different boats as he can manage. My own advice, based on many years as a sea kayaker and designer of sea kayaks, is presented in the sections that follow.

Hull Shape. A good hull shape is, of course, vital for sustained high speeds. The best hulls are from twenty-one to twenty-four inches wide and fifteen to seventeen feet long and are designed with a bottom shape that runs straight and tracks well even in a quartering sea aft. Any turning or correcting is done by leaning the kayak over onto its broadest section amidships and sweeping the paddle blade out far enough on the forward paddle stroke to bring the boat back around onto its correct heading.

An important factor governing speed in choppy conditions is the shape of the bow. Bow shapes can be of two designs: the very buoyant design that rides over normal-sized oncoming waves or one designed to slice and not plunge through the waves. The former works well except when seas are very steep and cause the bow to plunge and displace the water violently sideways. The displaced water then falls back and collides on the foredeck. The resulting clapotis (collision of waves)—a couple of feet from the bow—hits the forward-moving paddler in the face.

The slicing bow, on the other hand, cuts through the wave, throwing very little water sideways, and has a foredeck shaped to allow the bow to rise cleanly from the wave. A good slicing bow does not work solely through lack of buoyancy at the fore-end, as this will cause the kayak to submarine, but rather by careful planning and design.

No matter how designed, the bow should be fine (or narrow) enough to promote a smooth laminar flow of water over the forepart of the hull. The stern is also very important. This, too, should be fine, thereby minimizing any drag brought about by water separation. The stern also should be high enough to balance any windage the bow might receive and to prevent the otherwise good feature of a powerful bow from being blown downwind.

Wood and fabric folding boats, which are wide and flat-bottomed, are naturally very stable on flat water. Unfortunately, they tend to follow the angle of the water beneath them—rather disconcerting if the seas are steep. When paddling these kayaks in rough seas or breaking waves, most paddlers prefer to meet the seas head on because the design precludes any techniques other than those of a very basic kind. For this reason I consider these boats to belong to a branch of our sport apart from that of the modern fiber glass ocean kayak.

Cockpits. In the modern kayak, the coastlines for which designs have been intended have had a major impact on cockpit size. The coastline of Great Britain is virtually unprotected and open to large swells and sudden storms. Because of this, British designers have made their cockpits comparable in size to those of white water boats. Cockpits any smaller than this depend on the relative heights of the fore- and reardecks. Some of the skin boats from Greenland and Labrador, for example, have foredecks higher than the reardecks. The difference in height between the fore- and reardecks makes entry (and exit) quite easy; to enter one simply has to sit on the reardeck and slide into the cockpit with the legs straight.

Many of the boats designed in North America, in contrast, have fore- and reardecks of the same height (or nearly the same height; see fig. 3). Because of this, the cockpit openings are, of necessity, very large. Many of these boats are intended for paddlers who wish to explore relatively protected coastlines. In the Pacific Northwest, for example, the coastline that extends from Puget Sound to Glacier Bay, Alaska, has thousands of miles of islands, deep fjords, and a generally contorted coastline. A lifetime could be spent paddling this coastline without ever having to face the rigors and stresses of the open sea. In such cases, kayaks with large cockpits are perhaps adequate.

On the other hand, if one wishes to paddle unprotected coastlines or to be safe in the event of sudden violent storms, kayaks with large cockpits are, in my considered opinion, risky. Ideally, the ocean paddler should be supported in much the same way as the river paddler; he should have support at the

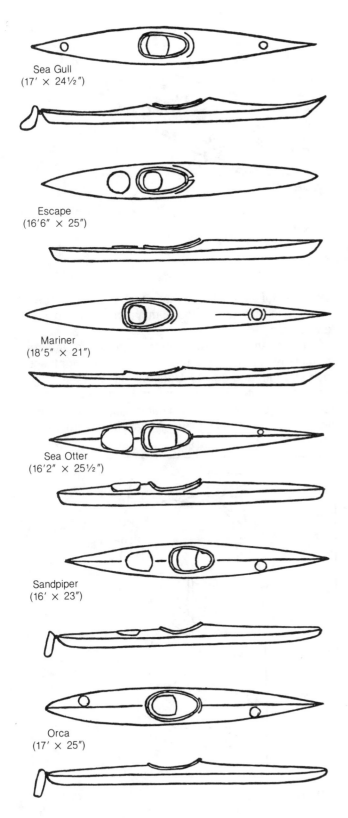

Sea Gull
(17' × 24½")

Escape
(16'6" × 25")

Mariner
(18'5" × 21")

Sea Otter
(16'2" × 25½")

Sandpiper
(16' × 23")

Orca
(17' × 25")

3. North American designs.

feet, knees, thighs, and seat. In a large cockpit it is often impossible to brace the knees. This deficiency is sometimes compounded by a poorly designed and loosely fitting seat, one that resembles a tiny armchair and offers no support to the thighs. Paddlers who own such boats can to an extent compensate by the addition of specially cut pieces of closed-cell foam carefully positioned and glued in place with contact cement.

Some cockpits are so large that the designers have given their kayaks sliding seats. The idea is to allow the paddler to trim the boat by sliding his weight back and forth. That the trim can be altered is no doubt true, but it can be argued that it is more advantageous to have a secure seat in a well-planned position that enables the paddler to brace himself and apply good technique to his corrective paddling strokes.

To allow the spray cover to fit snugly but safely, the cockpit coaming should be at least three-fourths inches wide and have sufficient clearance to allow a person's fingers to run around between it and the deck without jamming. The spray cover should fit tightly around the cockpit coaming and be in a good state of repair. Because the cover fits tightly, the release strap should be secure and efficient. One foolproof method is to afix with fiber glass a piece of webbing tape (approximately one foot long) underneath the deck just in front of the cockpit. Fit a loop or toggle to the end and lead this out of the cockpit and onto the top of the deck. No matter how tight the spray cover, it will come off with one pull without damage. After all, it is no good wrenching hard on a release strap only to have the strap pull off with the spray cover still in place. Did I say foolproof? Do not forget to place the release straps on the *outside* before putting on the spray cover.

Hatches and Bulkheads. The greatest innovation in ocean kayak design in recent years has been the introduction of watertight hatches and bulkheads. (See fig. 4; hatches are also discussed under deck layout.) Equipment can be kept dry at all times and the boat is virtually unsinkable. Any hatch that allows entry into the interior of a kayak should be watertight and designed so that it cannot be knocked off or displaced during deep-water rescues or when breaking seas crash across the deck. Some kayaks,

4. Cutaway section of the Ice Floe sea kayak shows water-tight hatches and bulkheads.

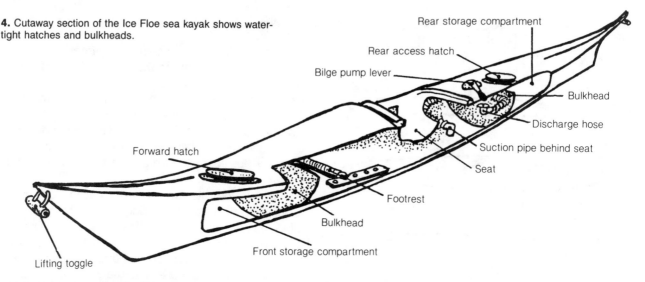

Rear storage compartment

Rear access hatch

Bilge pump lever

Bulkhead

Discharge hose

Suction pipe behind seat

Seat

Forward hatch

Footrest

Bulkhead

Front storage compartment

Lifting toggle

which manufacturers claim are designed for the ocean, exhibit hatches that are held in place by flimsy turn buttons, thin shock cord, or snap clips that would be better employed on a cheap suitcase than on an ocean-going craft. A kayak fitted in this manner should be viewed with suspicion. There is nothing wrong with a large hatch opening, so long as it remains watertight.

A small bilge pump can be fitted where it will not interfere with normal paddling, but most manufacturers place them on the reardeck just aft of the cockpit on either the left- or right-hand side. Also on the market now is an excellent foot-operated pump that is fixed to the footrest (the Lendal foot pump, fig. 5). Although this does not have the same discharge volume as the hand-operated version, it can be used without any interruption of the paddle stroke. I prefer to have both fitted just to be on the safe side.

Hull Strength and Weight. The decks of sea kayaks should be strong enough to support deep-water rescues or the weight of a distressed comrade if the need arises. Such stressful situations will soon show up the weakness in any design. Steve Sinclair, head guide and instructor of the Force 10 Ocean White Water Tours group, is accustomed to taking groups of people out to sea in rough conditions. He had this to say at the end of a training and rescue session I ran in a particularly exposed part of San Francisco Bay: "Most models could barely withstand the rigors of the various rescue procedures. The bottoms and decks cracked under the stress of basic rescue procedures. This demonstrated to me what I

have felt for some time: that most ocean kayaks I have seen are much too flimsy for actual ocean kayaking."

North American kayak manufacturers in particular have tended to place more emphasis on lightness than strength and rigidity. Until recently this has been a source of potential problems, but with the introduction of new and more sophisticated materials it is now possible to construct lightweight kayaks without sacri-

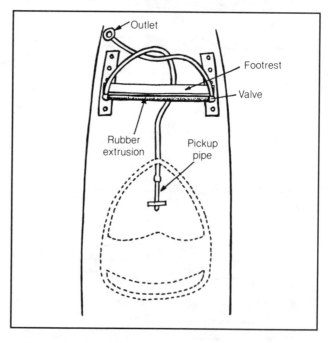

Outlet

Footrest

Valve

Rubber extrusion

Pickup pipe

5. The Lendal foot pump.

ficing the necessary strength. Make sure, however, that any lightweight model you consider purchasing has been thoroughly tested and can stand up under rescue conditions.

Another thing to consider when purchasing a lightweight kayak is that sea kayaks must have sufficient weight to provide momentum when paddling in rough conditions. A kayak being paddled at a brisk speed over wave crests may regularly have as much as six or seven feet of its length hanging in the air. If a strong wind is pressing against the beam of a featherweight kayak, the paddler could lose control. To be seaworthy in high winds and the accompanying sea conditions, an unladen kayak should weigh between fifty and sixty pounds.

It is possible to add weight to keep a lightweight kayak manageable in rough seas and high winds. This added weight must not move around inside the hull. Use long, narrow equipment bags, which are held in place against the bottom of the hull by loops of shock cord. These bags should be secured in position when the kayak is near the water's edge and must be distributed evenly fore and aft.

Plastic Sea Kayaks.　Plastic white-water kayaks have been with us now for almost a decade and a half, and over the last few years plastic sea-touring designs have been available, too.

What do we know of polyethylene as a material for boats from the long experience of the white-water paddler? The following table compares polyethylene with fiberglass.

	Polyethylene (Linear and Cross-Linked)	Fiberglass
Stiffness	Poor	Fair
Weight	Heavy	Medium
Abrasion Resistance	Poor	Fair
Impact Resistance	Very Good	Fair
Price	Inexpensive	Moderately expensive

I list linear and cross-linked polyethylene together here, as they are much more similar to each other than they are to fiberglass. Cross-linked polyethylenes are somewhat superior to linear, but unlike the latter, they cannot be repaired by welding.

So how do plastic sea kayaks hold up compared with conventional fiberglass boats? Not too well, I'm afraid.

Remember that the development of short white-water designs in vogue at present was partly triggered by the poor stiffness characteristics of polyethylene. But heavy use of block buoyancy within these kayaks was needed to prevent oil-canning (flexing of the hull) and serious wrap-arounds (jackknifing of the hull) associated with rocky river descents.

Sea-touring kayaks have more volume and are longer than white-water boats but are not subjected to the heavy bending forces encountered in white water—as long as they are kept out of the surf, that is! Even so, they need to have thick skins, which means extra weight. The metal rods and plastic stiffeners I see within most plastic sea kayaks tell me that there are stiffness problems still awaiting an elegant solution.

One problem that does not affect white-water kayaks, which are "stripped-down" craft, is the difficulty of effectively adding extra pieces to plastic boats. I am thinking particularly of bulkheads, which can be made watertight so easily in fiberglass boats but have presented insuperable difficulties in plastic. I have yet to see a bulkhead in a plastic boat that did not leak. It may not leak at first perhaps, but I overheard a well-known designer of plastic sea kayaks jokingly say, "I guarantee our bulkheads will leak within a month." On reflection, it didn't seem so funny.

One of the joys of owning a sea kayak is being able to customize one's own craft beyond the mere addition of extra bulkheads and hatches. I am thinking of such features as extra recessed deck-line fittings, anchor points for towlines, knee tubes, and compass wells, as well as other bits and pieces that make any nonkayaking months a time for innovation and experiment. This pleasure is denied to the owners of plastic boats.

Add to this the poor abrasion resistance of polyethylene and its lack of aesthetic appeal and you are left only with its price to commend it. Even this is not so competitive when you examine prices of fully fitted-out boats complete with rudders, skegs, hatches, deck-lines, compass housings, and so on. The cost of fitting this equipment to plastic and fiberglass boats is roughly the same.

I doubt whether an experienced sea-paddler would seriously contemplate owning a plastic boat, but the outfitter, watching his novice group hurling his boats against a stone jetty in a short chop, will be offering up a silent prayer of thanks to the scientist who invented polyethylene.

One word of caution: Research moves apace,

and more progress is being made with unsupported plastics (including polyethylene) than with reinforced plastics (fiberglass).

While I think it is fair to say that plastic sea kayaks are not yet up to the high standards of design and construction now expected of fiberglass craft, new materials will be discovered and new manufacturing processes will be invented. In fact, these processes are here now, but the costs are prohibitive. As costs inevitably fall, the sea-kayaking world will be able to take advantage of them, and the gap between the quality of plastic and fiberglass will narrow.

Rudders.   Paddlers often discuss whether kayaks should have rudders, and often the decision depends upon the kayak design. Some kayaks are specifically designed not to need a rudder. For example, the Baidarka Explorer (see fig. 6), which I designed, has a ridge or keelson that runs the full length of the boat. This enables the boat to grip the water in much the same way an ice skate locks itself onto the ice.

Rudders are undoubtedly an advantage for other kayak designs. To use another of my designs as an example of this type of boat, the Umnak (see fig. 7), which is only fifteen and a half feet long and has a rockered hull (a hull that slopes upward from the middle toward the bow and stern), has been fitted with a rudder by some owners. This helps the boat handle better in windblown, choppy seas.

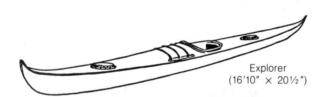

Explorer
(16'10" × 20½")

6. The keelson on the Baidarka Explorer (designed by the author) enables the boat to grip the water like an ice skate locking itself onto the ice. This design makes a rudder unnecessary.

Umnak
(15'5" × 24")

7. The Umnak (designed by the author) can be fitted with a rudder for use on the open sea.

Track deviation in a double kayak is also probably best corrected by using a rudder. This does away with the necessity of leaning the boat over onto one side, which is much more difficult with two paddlers than one.

Most single paddlers who depend on rudders at the beginning of their careers, however, tend to put them to one side as their skill level increases. For example, paddlers usually learn quickly that most ocean kayaks can be turned easily in bumpy seas by taking advantage of the waves and using the paddle: the boat is spun around by the paddle as the hull pirouettes around on the top of the waves.

Up to the time of this writing, rudders are rarely used by experienced British paddlers. It is generally held that they are more of a bother than they are worth. They get fouled up in nets or lines, inhibit seal landings and launchings, and always seem to snap, break, or bend at the worst possible time. However, with the recent emergence of rudder designs incorporating new materials, it appears that rudders will be more accepted.

If you do decide to use a rudder, be certain that you choose a good design. One of the best I have seen was designed by Chuck Sherburne for the Odyssea surf ski. Sherburne is a retired aerospace engineer, and his design exhibits the robust features that could be expected from someone who has been connected to that industry. His system requires very little pressure to turn the rudder, yet the footrest is solid on the heel for hard bracing during the normal paddling stroke. Steve Sinclair of the Force 10 unit has been using this type of rudder on his surf skis in all kinds of weather conditions for several years and has found them durable and effective.

Another excellent rudder mechanism (see fig. 8) was designed by Frank Goodman. Goodman based his design on a homemade affair used by Paul Caffyn on his epic circumnavigation of Australia. Known as the C-Trim rudder, the whole unit is fastened to a wedge which in turn is either bonded within the stern of the kayak's hull or to some external molding, customized to suit the shape of any kayak. The rudder and its molding could be held in place by wing nuts. For the owner who doesn't mind the trauma of sawing the stern off a favorite boat, the C-Trim can be fitted to most kayaks by simply trimming off the stern plate to fit the cross section of the boat. The rudder is made from moldings in polycarbonate and ABS, which support a fiberglass blade controlled by a foot pedal. The mechanism is fastened to the wedge-shaped block by two M8 setscrews. The fitting instructions are easy to follow and the whole affair is available in kit form to fit most boats. I have looked at the design closely and it is one of the few I think will stand up to a good deal of use or abuse.

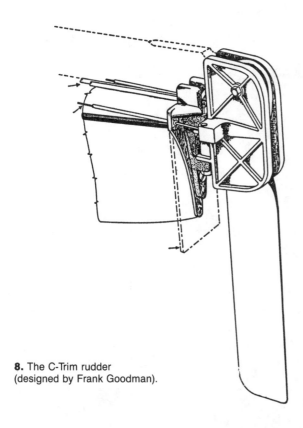

8. The C-Trim rudder (designed by Frank Goodman).

Deck Layout. Everyone involved in ocean touring seems to have his own pet way of rigging out a deck, but one of the most popular systems is shown in figure 9.

Plastic toggles (or homemade wooden toggles) are the most comfortable way to carry a kayak. They are also the safest to use when towing a kayak to shore after the misfortune of capsizing outside the surf line. Loops can twist around and trap fingers during the struggle to reach shore. Always check toggles to make sure that the knots inside are secure and the rope ends are heat sealed—a job often neglected by some manufacturers.

All equipment carried inside a kayak must be kept dry. Access to the storage compartments is gained by means of watertight hatches. At present, there are two designs favored by touring kayakers. The lid of Frank Goodman's recently designed hatch is made of strong, flexible plastic. This lid fits snugly onto a rigid rim, which can be either bolted onto the kayak or bonded directly into the deck of the boat during manufacturing. A retaining band of stainless steel, which is located in a recess running around the lid, is tensioned by an overcenter finger lock. The Henderson hatch is made of strong, rigid plastic and has a cleverly designed screw top lid that allows the outer rim to turn while the center portion of the lid remains still. The threads must be kept free from sand and grit to insure smooth movement. Releasing the lid with cold hands can be a problem, but paddlers usually overcome this with a simple home-made wooden bar spanner that rests across the lid and grips the lugs around the edge. No matter what type of hatch is used, the lids are less likely to become lost if they are painted a bright color or fastened to the inside of the hull with a long string. When tightening screw hatches, take care not to start on a cross thread. If any long items of equipment such as a rifle or fishing rod are to be carried, then a third hatch fitted in the forward bulkhead will make storage easy.

The paddle park prevents the paddle from wandering away during filming, rescuing, fishing, or eating. The one I use started life as a broom clip.

Grab lines around the deck should be tight and stay that way. Some like to have grab lines around the reardeck, but I do not think this is necessary. Tensioning is also useful for fastening a kayak to a car's roof rack.

The chart table and compass are held by shock cords. Some paddlers prefer to have their compass more forward and to house it in custom-built deck recesses.

Recessed deck fittings keep the grab lines close to the deck. With no protrusions there is less possibility of damage or injury during deep-water rescues. If your kayak has an inadequate number of deck fittings, figure 10 details a method of creating your own.

The small bilge pump can be fitted for either right- or left-hand use. The suction hose can be extra long so that the paddler can help others empty out their boats if necessary.

The towline is a very important item of emer-

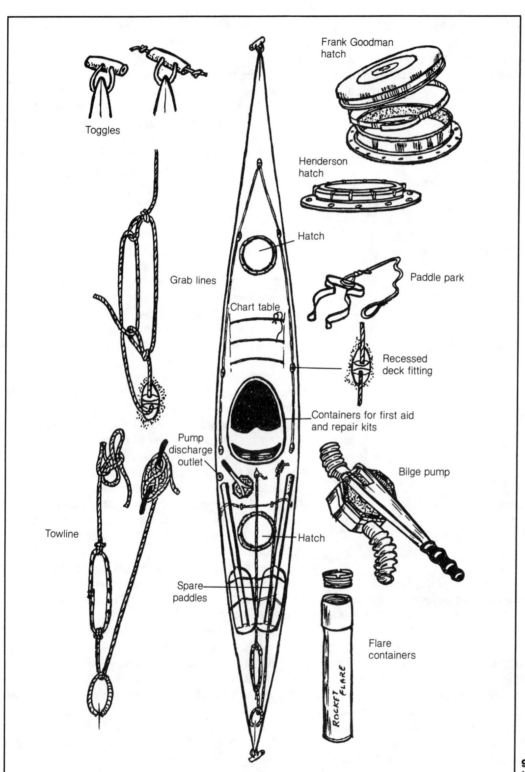

Toggles

Frank Goodman
hatch

Henderson
hatch

Hatch

Grab lines

Paddle park

Chart table

Recessed
deck fitting

Containers for first aid
and repair kits

Pump
discharge
outlet

Bilge pump

Towline

Hatch

Spare
paddles

ROCKET FLARE

Flare
containers

9. A popular deck layout
for sea touring.

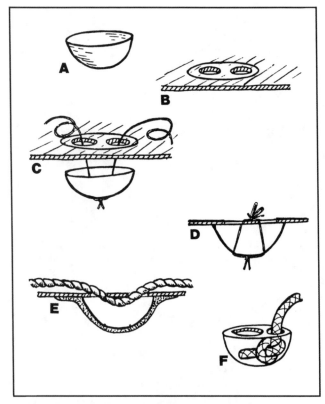

10. Recessed deck fitting.
Make a small cup by cutting a table-tennis ball in half and reinforcing it with a square of fiberglass mat where the holes will be drilled (A). Trace a circle on the deck where the cup is to be placed and drill two holes inside the circle (B). To hold the cup in place, pass a piece of strong thread through two pinholes pricked in the cup. Lead the thread through the holes in the deck (C). Tightly tie the thread to secure the cup (D). Turn the boat upside down and apply a piece of resin-soaked fiberglass mat over the cup. As soon as the fiberglass hardens, deck line can be passed through the two holes (E). If the fitting is to be used for deck shock cord elastics, make one of the holes large enough for the knot to pass through (F).

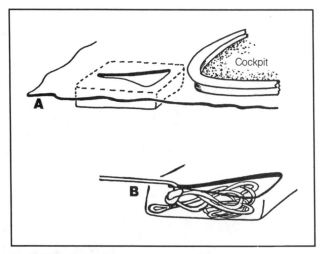

11. Stuff box for towline.
Make a stuff box using the same method as in figure 10. The box shape is made from thin cardboard, which is glued or taped together and then covered with fiberglass matting (A). When the fiberglass has hardened, the cardboard liner can be left to rot away. A slot, which is wide at one end and tapered at the other, should be cut into the deck. The end of the towline is held in position by the knot that slides into the tapered slot (B). A loop of shock cord, which forms part of the towline, provides enough tension to keep the line in place. The box holds the remaining three to four feet of line.

gency equipment. It is best to anchor it just behind the cockpit with either a jam cleat or a rope loop fiberglassed into the deck. Use a quick-release knot. The line is then passed through a spliced eye or one made from plastic at the stern and led forward again to terminate at some convenient point just behind the cockpit. Everyone seems to have a favorite system for towline arrangement. My own system of anchoring the free end of the towline is by means of a stuff box (fig. 11), but whichever system is used should be one that can be employed quickly and cause no danger to the person towing, should he accidentally capsize. Al-

though nylon rope will stretch with the strain of towing, a loop of shock cord can be incorporated into the towline, so as to relieve any sudden shocks that may occur when the line is used in rough weather. Shock cord is best joined by a fisherman's knot or by using crimps made from stainless steel. To keep the elastic from snapping and parting the line, the shock cord should be fixed across a loop in the line, so that even if the elastic gives out the rope is still in one piece.

Spare paddles are carried on the reardeck held on by tightly stretched shock cord.

The discharge outlet for the pump is positioned so that the discharged water does not shoot up the arm of the operator.

Flare containers can be made of plumbers' plastic waste pipe. I carry my flares under the same elastics as the spare paddles. Paint the containers fluorescent orange and make a note of the expiration date of the flares.

Containers holding the first aid and repair kit are in the space behind the seat. A sponge should be carried under the seat to help keep the boat clean and dry.

EQUIPMENT

Basic Equipment

Paddles.   During those far-off days when my wood and canvas PBK 10 (an early kayak) and I were inseparable, I used to paddle out to sea using a nicely varnished pair of all wooden paddles joined in the center with a shiny brass ferrule. When this paddle stood next to me on the ground, the top of it was almost lost in the clouds. It had to be long because, although the boat I paddled was only slightly over ten feet long, it was thirty-three inches wide, and a paddle any shorter would have meant leaving the best part of my knuckles on the gunwale.

As kayaks became narrower, paddles became shorter. Since the sea paddler had no guideline for determining the best paddle length for these narrow kayaks, he used the river paddler's standard as a guide. By this standard, the paddler should be able to reach up and hook his fingers over the top of the blade when the paddle is standing upright in front of him.

To be most effective, a paddle must possess certain qualities. It should be comfortable to hold, and it should be strong. In order to minimize turbulence, the blade must enter the water smoothly without creating any splash. When a paddle enters the water, any splashing is energy wasted. Curved blades enter the water without disturbing the surface, and an asymmetrical curved blade will do this even more smoothly. Once the blade is immersed, any air around the blade—shown by white bubbles—will re-duce its efficiency. Air is dragged down as the paddle enters the water. This is more noticeable around the back of the blade. Once in the water, a paddle blade must create drag—it must grip the water. The surface area of the blade is a crucial factor here. The most efficient are called "spoon blades." These are curved laterally as well as longitudinally. The very curve that gives the propulsion, however, is too great to allow the blade to slice in and out of the sea without splash.

It is propelled by a two-bladed paddle, which is held in the middle and dipped in the water on each side in turn, like the paddles we use in canoes. It has probably been developed from the Indians' one-bladed paddles. Among the Eskimos on the southwest coast of Alaska the one-bladed paddle is universal; not until we come north of the Yukon River do we find two-bladed paddles, and even there the single blade is still the more common. Further north and eastward along the American coast both forms are found, until the two blades at last come into exclusive use eastward of the Mackenzie River.

The Aleutians seem, strangely enough, to be acquainted with only the two-bladed paddle, and this is also the case, so far as I can gather, with the Asiatic Eskimos. (Nansen, Eskimo Life, pp. 48–49.)

Because of this, a compromise has to be reached and the curves are reduced so that both operations are provided for.

Although curved blades do well at creating little splash, they do have more tendency than paddles with other shapes to flutter. Fluttering is caused by the eddies and vortices that break away from the edge of the blade. Alternately, vortices break away from the edge and cause pressures to build up on the face of the blade. Because the face of the blade cannot make way against the pressures, the paddle will begin to move quickly from side to side—or flutter. Fluttering reduces the efficiency of the stroke and can be disturbing because the paddle feels unsteady in the hand.

Curved blades are more efficient than any other kind of paddle for the high racing stroke. But in a strong beam wind, a long, thin paddle is less likely to be caught by severe gusts. This is because the long, thin paddle can be completely immersed in the water at a more acute angle and the upper blade is consequently lower during the stroke. For this reason, the long, thin blade is the type of paddle I prefer. My paddling colleagues are divided in their preferences between the long, thin paddle (such as the Seamaster) and the asymmetric curved paddle (such as the Nordcapp).

Paddle weight is as important as paddle length. Paddles should be light as well as strong in order to withstand many hours of use. I like a paddle that has sufficient weight to maintain momentum during the forward stroke. I also favor a shaft that flexes slightly. To make paddling more comfortable and to give a more positive grip on the shaft during an Eskimo roll, the shaft should have a slightly oval shape where the hands grip and are at right angles to the nearest blade.

Paddle Leash. The paddle leash (fig. 12) is an indispensable means of keeping paddle and paddler together. A paddle leash of thin shock cord is simple to make, and it can be worth its weight in gold. No matter what the circumstances or how rough the sea, the paddle will never become parted from the paddler. To join the elastic, simply crimp it together with precut pieces of stainless steel or bind it with twine.

Clothing. Kayaking on the sea is a dry sport—or so I keep trying to tell everybody. However, novices do get wet. On the bottom half, beginners

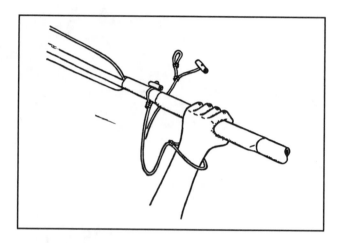

12. The paddle leash.

should wear high-waisted wet suit trousers made of three to four millimeter neoprene or long johns that have shoulder straps. On the top half, they should wear any warm, comfortable clothing. Fiberpile is very popular, but whatever is chosen must be kept dry by a waterproof anorak. Some years ago, I designed one based on an Inuit hunter's kayak smock, and it has proved very popular.

Full wet suit jackets can cause chafing and fatigue. Novices who insist on wearing one should make sure there is plenty of room around the armpits or cut the arms out altogether.

Feet should be protected from the cold and wet, but the footwear chosen should also be solid enough to allow the kayaker to walk comfortably over stones or slippery rocks during landings. Most experienced paddlers wear loose fitting Wellington boots with warm socks. They have also discarded neoprene trousers for something more comfortable. I wear track suit bottoms made of double force material and covered by high-waisted waterproof sailing trousers.

The decision to cast off sweaty neoprene gear for the comfort of fiberpile and waterproofs is a serious one that should be made only by experienced paddlers. If there is the remotest chance of being immersed in cold water, stay with the neoprene.

Pogies. Cold hands can make paddling uncomfortable, and in cold weather the experience can be almost unbearable. Gloves are not completely satisfactory because they tend to destroy the feel for the paddle shaft. There are a number of solutions. Neoprene Smittens (fig. 13) can be used. These are made

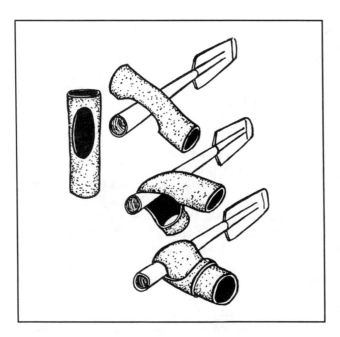

13. Neoprene Smittens designed by Frank Goodman.

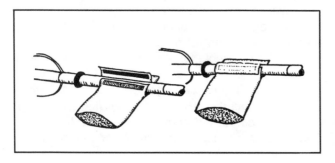

14. Muffins protect the hands from cold winds without constricting the wrist.

by Valley Canoe Products in Britain. The simpler muffins (fig. 14) are equally satisfactory. Both of these items fall into the general category of pogies.

Headgear. Headgear is important, and what you wear depends very much on what you are going to do and where you intend to do it. Most paddlers wear crash helmets for surfing, but in cold weather these can also be worn over a neoprene hat for extra warmth. It is sometimes advisable to wear a crash helmet for deepwater rescue practices, especially when these are conducted in rough conditions. For normal paddling in cold weather, a wool hat can provide the necessary protection or the hood of an anorak can be worn over a large peaked truckers' hat.

In fair weather the kaiak-man uses the so-called half-jacket (akuilisak). This is made of water-tight skin with the hair removed, and is sewn with sinews. Round its lower margin runs a draw-string, or rather a draw thong, by means of which the edge of the jacket can be made to fit so closely to the kaiak-ring that it can only be pressed and drawn down over it with some little trouble. This done, the half-jacket forms, as it were, a watertight extension of the kaiak. The upper margin of the jacket comes close up to the armpits of the kaiak-man. . . .

Loose sleeves of skin are drawn over the arms, and are lashed to the overarm and to the wrist, thus preventing the arm from becoming wet. Watertight mittens of skin are drawn over the hands. This half-jacket is enough to keep out the smaller waves which wash over the kaiak. In a heavier sea, on the other hand, the whole-jacket (tuilik) is used. This is made in the same way as the half-jacket, and, like it, fits close to the kaiak-ring, but is longer above, has sleeves attached to it, and a hood which comes right over the head. It is laced tight round the face and wrists, so that with it on the kaiak-man can go right through the breakers and can capsize and right himself again, without getting wet and without letting a drop of water into the kaiak. (Nansen, Eskimo Life, pp. 49–51.)

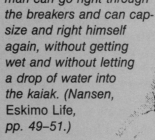

The large peak gives excellent facial protection when paddling head into wind and is very similar in its protection qualities to the peaked headgear worn by the old-time Aleuts when they were engaged in sea otter hunting. Too much sun can be dangerous, and the reflection off the water can even burn the lips. Choose a hat therefore that gives protection all around from the hot sun. If the heat of the sun causes overheating, it is time well spent to stop and remove a few layers of clothing.

Poncho. A poncho keeps off the rain and, at the same time, allows air to circulate and prevents condensation. One that can double as a bivouac tent is useful in survival situations and also makes changing out of wet clothes in the open a bearable experience. Choose one that is a bright fluorescent color to double as a rescue marker.

Personal Flotation Devices. The only suitable personal flotation device (PFD) is the life jacket which, unlike the buoyancy aid, is designed to float the head of an unconscious person above water. All beginners should wear a life jacket at *all* times. Because of the awkward and ungainly shape of some PFDs that have integral buoyancy already included inside, most experienced paddlers wear buoyancy aids that do not have any self-righting facility. On long trips in calm seas and in the company of others, the experienced paddler may not wear a buoyancy aid, but carries it within easy reach under deck elastics to be worn for difficult landings or when weather conditions are bad. A cautionary word about life jackets: if they are worn with trousers made of neoprene, the buoyancy effect of the trousers will cause legs and feet to rise to the surface and thus cancel the self-righting quality of the life jacket.

Life Deck. The first edition of this book featured a description of the life deck. This is no longer produced and has therefore been omitted from this edition. It was banned by the International Canoe Federation (ICF) because it gave no upper-body protection to river kayakers.

Waterproof Bags and Containers. Any equipment stowed inside a kayak *must stay dry—* survival could depend on it. The salt water that seeps into worn, badly tied, or poorly repaired waterproof bags and ruins clothing, food supplies, sleeping bags and cameras, could be fatal to anyone involved in an extended sea trip. It also could be an intolerable burden on the rest of the party. In a situation where individuals carry items of a special nature, to be used by the rest of the group (medical supplies, cameras and film, radio equipment and, in some instances, firearms and ammunition), any loss or damage could blunt the efficiency of the group and may put them in grave danger.

Any bag or container can be used as long as it can be opened and closed repeatedly without damage. Good serviceable bags can be made from ex-army capes and groundsheets. The plastic bags commonly used to carry garden and kitchen rubbish are hardly suitable. I prefer to use bags that are specially designed to fit through the deck hatch openings. Naturally, if your kayak has one of the smaller hatches, you must be prepared to transfer items such as sleeping bags and tents into these new narrow bags. With these bags packing for a long trip may take a little more time, but care and consideration are a small price to pay for dry gear.

Equipment carried inside watertight compartments also should be protected inside waterproof bags, just in case a rock or other object puts a hole in the kayak.

All bags and containers should be made secure so that in the event of a capsize they stay with the boat and do not entangle the paddler in long, untidy securing lines.

First Aid and Emergency Kits. An emergency repair kit (fig. 15) and a small first aid kit (fig. 16) should be carried permanently inside the kayak. These items should be adequate for day trips and short jaunts.

Figure 17 is a first aid kit for an extended trip. The items listed should suffice for four to six people for a two-month trip. Also include any items of a specialist nature, which would normally be carried in the small kit, such as the Brooks airway (fig. 18). For some areas it may be necessary to include snake bite serum. Complete the first aid kit with a copy of an up-to-date first aid book.

For British travelers, the normally generous National Health Service does not supply medication for trips abroad (other than for a preexisting medical condition), and all drugs needed for this purpose have to be purchased—usually at a considerably greater expense than anticipated. Friendly doctors, usually general practitioners, may defray this expense by donating drug samples. Travelers should otherwise ask their doctor to sign the entire list as a private pre-

Swiss Army knife	Epoxy glue
Copper wire	Sharpening stone
Pliers	Plastic bag containing toilet
Precut stainless steel clips (for joining shock cord elastic)	paper and coins
	Waterproof torch
	Firelighting tablets
Cord (for spare bow loop)	Signaling mirror
Patches or duct tape	Fishing line
Adhesive	Fishhooks and weight
Scissors	Small can opener
Sail needle	Coil of thin, strong line
Terylene thread	Heavy-duty polyethylene
Sailors palm	exposure bag
Waterproof matches	Patch kit (resin, catalyst,
Candle stump	and fiberglass mat)
Bottle of acetone	

15. Essential items for an emergency repair kit.

Assorted bandaids	Antibacterial ointment
Assorted bandages (ace, triangular, etc.)	Antihistamine cream
	Sun protection
Adhesive tape	Snake bite serum
Gauze roll	Scissors
Water purification tablets	Tweezers
Aspirin	Safety pins
Seasickness pills	Plastic tubing and an airway (such as a Brooks airway)
Pain killer	
Antiseptic cream	First aid book

16. Items to be included in a small first aid kit.

scription. American travelers should also obtain drugs on prescription; in some cases it is illegal to buy or possess them without prescription.

Be sure to take along the prescriptions or photocopies of their descriptions for the drugs (with indication, recommended dosage). In the United States all drugs are listed in *The Physician's Desk Reference,* published annually.

Store the kit in waterproof containers and transfer liquids and tablets into plastic bottles (except for one glass bottle for sting suction) and attach labels with tape because stick-on labels can come off in wet heat. The kit should be accessible at all times and at least one person should be thoroughly familiar with the contents of the kit, knowing the exact location of each item.

Climbing Rope. A climbing rope is useful for lowering kayaks and equipment down cliffs and essential for rescue purposes in the event of glacier

Basic Kit
Dressings
  Adhesive bandages (50 assorted sizes)
  Elastic bandages (two, 3″ × 5′)
  Butterfly bandages (assorted sizes)
  Gauze rolls (one, 2″ and one, 3″)
  Triangular bandage (one, 40″)
  Gauze squares (twelve, 3″ × 3″ and twelve, 4″ × 4″)
  Compresses (assorted)
  Adhesive tape (two rolls, one, 2″ and one, 3″)
  Cotton wool pack (compressed)

Cleansing
  Bar soap or mild disinfectant

Instruments
  Scissors (2 pair, blunt and sharp)
  Forceps (1 pair)
  Sterile scalpel blade (1)
  Safety pins (4)
  Thermometers (2)
  Disposable syringes and needles
  Suture material
  Paper and ballpoint pen (to note drugs given)

Medicines
  Aspirin or acetaminophen (50 tablets)
  Painkillers*
  Antibiotics*
  Sedatives*
  Antihistamines*
  Diarrhea medications*
  Laxatives*
  Coated sodium (20 tablets)
  Antiworm medication*
  Anti-inflammatory eye and eardrops*

Oil of cloves for toothache
Temporary tooth filling material**

Topical medications
  Sunscreen (2 tubes)
  Zinc oxide ointment or Vaseline
  Lip balm with sunscreen (1 tube)
  Calamine cream (1 tube)
  Insect repellent
  Lotrimin ointment for fungal infections (1 tube)
  Mercurochrome or tincture of iodine
  Louse or insect powder
  Anusol for hemorrhoids (10 suppositories)
  Antimalarial medication***
  Rubbing alcohol

Individual kit
Dressings
  Adhesive bandages (assorted sizes)
  Gauze bandages (3″ × 3″)

Instruments
  Razor blade
  Paper and ballpoint pen (to note drugs given)

Medicines
  Aspirin or acetaminophen (12 tablets)
  Antibiotics*
  Personal prescriptions*
  Diarrhea medications*
  Anti-inflammatory eye and eardrops*
  Iodine-based water purifying tablets (100)

Topical medications
  Sunscreen (1 tube)
  Zinc oxide ointment or Vaseline
  Lip balm with sunscreen

  * Consult a physician for specific prescriptions.
 ** Consult a dentist to obtain.
*** Consult a physician for medication appropriate to the area you are traveling through.

17. A basic first aid kit for an extended trip.

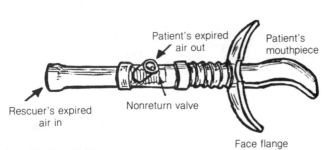

Patient's expired
air out

Patient's
mouthpiece

Rescuer's expired
air in

Nonreturn valve

Face flange

18. The Brooks airway

19. The pod.

walking. Although the rope will be heavy and bulky, it can be carried slung under the deck between a paddler's legs. Wrap the rope in a polyethylene bag to keep it in good condition.

Fog Horn. Do not bother with the gas-operated fog horn—it never seems to work when most needed. The best and most reliable fog horn is lung-operated. Little can go wrong with it and the blast is quite ear-shattering. Make sure the fog horn is fastened to the kayak by a long cord.

Fog horns are used for the following:
- To signal groups on land.
- To control groups on the water.
- To frighten bears.
- To make a distress call.
- To avoid being run down in busy shipping lanes under foggy conditions. Sounding the signal "D"—*one long blast and two short blasts*—will let vessels know that you maneuver with difficulty, and they should keep clear.

Special Equipment

The Pod. For those who nurture the uncontrollable urge to paddle alone on the sea, an item of equipment worth considering is the pod (fig. 19).

The pod is a fiberglass capsule, designed by Alan Byde, that seals off the space needed by the paddler from the rest of the kayak's hull. In the event of a capsize, the water that enters the pod can be measured in pints rather than gallons. In fact, the pod limits the amount of water that enters the boat to such an extent that emptying the kayak and the rescues I describe in later chapters are totally unnecessary.

Like most good ideas, the pod was developed by trial and error. Byde was originally influenced by the

Chaussette, or kneeling bag, as used by C-1 and C-2 (one-man Canadian and two-man Canadian) whitewater paddlers. This canvas bag was secured to the manhole rim and gave the paddler a separate compartment sealed off from the main body of the hull. If the occupant was forced to leave the boat during a capsize, only the bag filled with water, and this was easily emptied by turning the bag inside out.

Applying this principle to a seagoing kayak, Byde first of all designed a fiberglass cockpit liner (fig. 20). It was made in two halves for easy fitting and consisted of a foot box and a bucket seat. The foot box was fitted into the kayak first and fiberglassed against the underside of the deck. The seat was fitted next by joining that molding to the foot box and then fiberglassing the upper rim of the seat molding around the underside of the cockpit. This liner could be installed in almost any fiberglass kayak and fit almost any size paddler (at least up to thirty-four inches of inside leg and size twelve shoe). Although the liner was easy to fit, a cockpit rim appropriate to the kayak was still required as a separate item. The additional weight of the liner, however, was negligible, and a

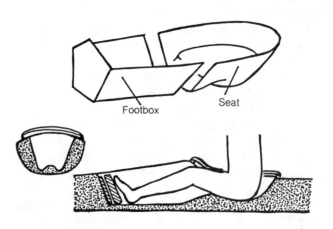

Footbox

Seat

20. The cockpit liner.

kayak fitted with a liner weighed approximately only half a kilo more than a boat fitted with a conventional seat, bulkheads, and footrest.

Unfortunately, for a number of reasons, the liner proved impracticable to market. The whole idea had to be rethought, and eventually the one-piece pod capsule was born. This self-contained unit has thigh braces to permit rolling, and the rim of the pod is attached to a mating rim on the kayak, which is formed inside the deck opening.

A pod or cockpit liner makes it possible to roll a kayak without the use of a spray cover. This is ideal if a reentry and roll have to be performed, as it makes emptying out afterward completely unnecessary.

The pod is shaped so that the cockpit almost empties itself completely when the kayak is leaned over on its side in the water. The stern of the boat also can be depressed so that the kayak tilts to an angle of about forty-five degrees, and the water drains out from the back of the cockpit.

After emptying, there may be a small amount of water left in the pod, but this does not affect the handling of the kayak. As the pod never takes on more than six gallons of water—unless you cheat and fill it with a bucket—even the weakest person or a very young child can maneuver the kayak into an emptying position.

The pod also reinforces the center section of the kayak. If the paddler has the misfortune of wrapping his kayak around a jetty support, fish trap, or tree, and the current is strong, the boat will not fold up around the paddler's legs amidships, thereby trapping him; it will shear off behind the cockpit.

Obviously a pod will not prevent a kayak from being wrecked, but it will allow the paddler to escape from the wreck.

Whether the pod becomes a popular addition to commercially built kayaks remains to be seen. At present, this undoubtedly safe accessory is available only if kayak owners are prepared to have one fitted as a separate item after they have purchased their boat. Looking back over the years, however, I can recall numerous instances where a great deal of sweat, heartache, and nervous tension could have been saved if my companions had possessed podded kayaks.

In 1988 a near tragedy on the Irish Sea highlighted a hitherto unforeseen problem. On a rough sea, a paddler became aware that a hole in the hull of his boat was causing it to take in large quantities of water. Before long his kayak, which was fitted with a pod, became unmanageable. Luckily for the paddler, his distress did not go unnoticed, and he was eventually winched to safety by a helicopter.

It became obvious that an accidental hole anywhere in the hull of a kayak so equipped would allow water to gain unrestricted entry into the main body of the sealed interior. Without the constraints of bulk-

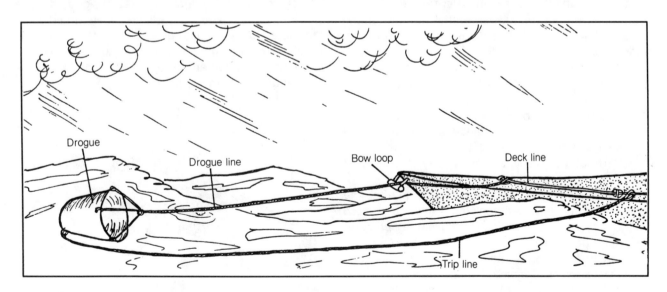

21. The drogue.

heads, and in any kind of swell, this uncontrolled water would swill from end to end, severely influencing the kayak's handling capabilities.

If water pours into a boat fitted with the usual bulkheads, the pressure builds until eventually no more water can get in. The air thus trapped, together with the buoyancy provided by the undamaged compartments, helps to keep the kayak and its occupant on the surface and mobile. If, however, the kayak has even the slightest leak above the waterline, the air will escape and the pressure will be lost, allowing more water to enter. Nevertheless, there will still be enough overall buoyancy in the kayak to support the paddler.

A leak above the waterline in a podded boat will, in like manner, cause air to escape, pressure to be lost, and more water to enter. Unfortunately, without bulkheads, the consequence may well be a fully swamped kayak. Even where a leak is small and air pressure loss is minimal, the water that enters will naturally slop from end to end of the hull with no bulkheads to limit or restrain it. Even if the kayak is not completely swamped, it will be extremely difficult to control in rough conditions.

The only practical way to get rid of the water inside a kayak fitted with a sealed cockpit liner is to remove the hatches prior to a deep-water rescue. The practice of removing hatches on the open sea has always been deplored for safety reasons. Even hatches secured by string and light chains have been torn away in the heat of rough-water rescues. For this reason, I design all my kayaks so that an unaccompanied paddler would find it almost impossible to remove his own hatches.

Of course, one has to be realistic and recognize that leaks are not restricted to podded boats. It may be necessary to empty water from the compartment of a kayak fitted with bulkheads. In this case, however, the open hatch does not lead into the main body of the kayak's hull, and even if the rescue goes badly, the horror of a complete swamping is not a constant threat.

Most leading kayak designers agree that the only way to make pods completely safe is to fit them with bulkheads. Until a better system emerges, I would support this conclusion.

Drogue. I can think of a number of situations when a paddler's discomfort might be eased if the bow of a kayak—whether for one paddler or two—can be maintained head to wind without any effort on the

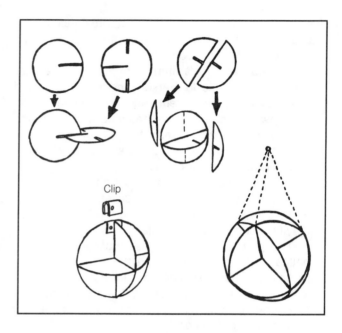

22. A radar reflector, made from sixteen S.W.G. (standard wire gauge) aluminum or aluminum alloy, will enable ships to detect the presence of a kayaker in a busy shipping lane.

part of the paddler. You may want either to keep dry and sit out a storm without undue drifting or to insure the stability of the kayak while fishing, eating, relieving yourself, flying your kite for pleasure not propulsion, or even snuggling down inside the hull to sleep. Whatever the reason, a strong, well-designed drogue (or sea anchor; see fig. 21) will create enough drag in the water to swing the bow or the stern into the weather—depending where the drogue is anchored. For instance, if you are flying a kite, it might be prudent to drogue from the stern.

23. The bang stick.

Once you have fitted your drogue, it would be wise to test it inside the surf line—a small surf will do fine. After all, how often do you get two-foot breaking seas on the open ocean?

Figure 21 shows a reliable design, which is less bothersome to handle than the multi-string parachute type. The drogue is made of a canvas-type material and is open at both ends. The line, of an overall length of approximately thirty feet, passes through the bow loop. The drogue line is fastened to the deck line and the end of the trip line is secured within easy reach.

Radar Reflector. It is not wise to play in busy shipping lanes. The danger of being run down in dense fog is great, especially by ships that travel fast or have difficulty in maneuvering. A radar reflector is a device used by boats of all sizes to reflect the radar waves given off by vessels which carry radar equipment as part of their navigational aids. If the reflector is hung in a prominent position it should enable shipping or rescue services to be aware of a paddler's presence in busy shipping areas.

If you want to make a long-lasting radar reflector that has a professional look, proceed as follows (see fig. 22).

Make the reflector from aluminum and be sure all the faces are at *right angles to each other at all times*. The higher the reflector is placed above sea level the better. Paint it fluorescent orange to increase visibility. Make it not less than eight inches in diameter. Suspend it by a strong cord in the "rain catching position," or so the apex of the three uppermost segments points downward, as illustrated. Remember that even a good reflector can be rendered useless when hung up incorrectly.

Reflectors made of aluminum can be a little cumbersome, however. An alternative is to lightly form some kitchen foil into a ball about nine inches in diameter and pack it in an open-mesh bag. Either hang this up on the end of a thin rod to increase the range or stick it under the reardeck elastics. I did some tests with the Northumbria River Police boat and discovered that with the foil I gave off a blip equal to that given off by quite a large fishing boat or a navigation buoy. This can keep morale high when it is foggy and there is a lot of traffic about.

Bang Stick. There are parts of the world where an attack by sharks could be high on the list of hazards faced by the kayak paddler. In such an area,

carrying a device known as a bang stick (fig. 23) is a useful precaution. (Also see discussion under Sharks in chapter on hazardous wildlife.)

A 12- or 20-gauge shotgun cartridge is contained in a special holder at the end of a long steel rod. A split pin holds the firing pin clear of the cartridge. The power head is made to fit over the point of a normal fish spear without threading.

To operate the bang stick, first remove the safety clip. Once this is done, the explosive charge is fired by pushing the power head against a firm surface. The effect is twofold: the prey is injured and it is also affected by the shockwave of the explosion.

There are two precautions worth taking: secure the safety clip so that it cannot become lost, and do not hold the bang stick in line with any part of your body. Unless the bang stick is completely submerged, the recoil will not be absorbed by the water.

Firearms. There are three reasons why it may be necessary to carry some kind of firearm with normal kayaking equipment: to kill to eat, to prevent something from eating you, or to protect yourself from other humans (fortunately, this applies only to some parts of the world). These usually will occur during expeditions to wilderness areas.

Killing to eat means filling a cooking pot and not, please note, filling a freezer. Because of this I give no instructions on how to kill a caribou.

To kill small animals and birds the best choice will be a good quality bolt action .22-caliber rifle. Bolt action weapons are traditionally reliable, accurate, and easy to repair and maintain. I do not recommend shooting small fry with .440-caliber Magnum repeating rifles, as there will be very little left to eat.

Animals that might eat you are usually also very large, and will move very quickly. Taking into consideration that you are probably not the world's best shot—especially when your hand is shaking with understandable anxiety—and that the animal has to be stopped at all costs, I would recommend the 12-gauge short-barreled shotgun loaded with a solid slug. It is a pump action weapon and can be fitted with a pistol grip and a folding stock. Because of its size when folded, it is ideal to store inside a kayak. Keep it in a waterproof bag and sling it underneath the foredeck between your knees.

During normal camp activities, the gun should be left in a place known to everyone, and it should be left in the same firing condition each time. You might keep it *loaded* with the *safety catch off*, but *without a round in the breech*. If it has to be fired in a hurry—one pump—then bang; there is no time wasted wondering if the safety catch is on or off or whether or not the gun needs cocking.

A few years ago a picture appeared on the front cover of *Canoeing* magazine showing Dr. Mike Jones crouching down next to his kayak loading a revolver. The photo was taken during an expedition he led down the Blue Nile and the weapon was used for protection against crocodiles and bandits. These bandits actually fired on him during the expedition and it brought home to me the fact that there are still remote parts of the world where travelers can be killed for no other reason than the food and medical supplies they carry. If research indicates that problems of this nature are likely to occur, seek advice from the appropriate government department in the country you intend to visit. Inquiries regarding the suitability of various types of weapons are best directed to local police or army units. If approached correctly, I have found both to be sympathetic and informative on the subject of firearms. Information from travelers who have already passed through the area you intend to visit also is invaluable. News in wilderness areas travels fast, and it will soon become known that you have taken precautions to defend yourself and that you would not be easy pickings for those who might have designs on your equipment.

You cannot be too careful with loaded firearms. Leaders of expeditions should make sure that members of the group have had proper weapon training, otherwise someone is going to have a foot blown off—or worse!

Revolvers should always be carried with one chamber empty, and that chamber should be the one next to the firing pin.

Rifles should never be cocked—i.e., a cartridge should not be fed into the breech—unless the gun is to be fired immediately.

Salt water and sweaty hands will ruin any firearm, so check, oil, and clean firearms daily.

Most ammunition is waterproof, and that includes shotgun cartridges, but any rounds that are stored in wet bags inside a kayak will start to corrode. Although this will not stop the round from being fired, it will probably stop it from being ejected because the empty cartridge will stick in the breech and thus render the gun useless after the first shot.

KAYAK STROKES AND MANEUVERS

Proficiency

Unlike folding boats, modern sea kayaks do not breed "instant" kayakers, and paddlers should master the techniques necessary to become proficient ocean kayakers. Let me define exactly what I consider a proficient sea kayaker.

As far as practical skills are concerned, the proficient paddler should be able to:

- Paddle a kayak out through at least four-foot breakers and into open water, then back in again, then forward and backward without capsizing.
- Tow the kayak ashore in the event of a capsize, and maintain contact not only with the kayak, but with the paddle and equipment.
- Turn a kayak around through 360 degrees using forward and reverse sweep strokes. This should be done as quickly as the design of the boat will allow.
- Move a kayak sideways by means of a draw stroke or a sculling draw stroke.
- Prevent a kayak from capsizing using a sculling for support stroke and also a slap support stroke.
- Steer a kayak with a stern rudder while traveling down the face of a small wave, then allow the kayak to come broadside on to a breaking wave and then, with a high brace, keep the boat upright as the wave breaks over it.
- Assist another kayaker in emptying out the kayak of a third person who has capsized and then put the person back in the boat.

All of the aforementioned strokes and maneuvers should be possible at this stage in moderate weather conditions—winds of Force 4 and a swell of five feet. I have not mentioned the Eskimo roll, as I consider that any proficient kayaker should not have to resort to this advanced maneuver in moderate weather conditions.

All proficient sea kayakers should have a sound knowledge of elementary seamanship including:

- The effect of tides and how to allow for them and the influence they have on the surface of the sea, having special regard to overfalls, rips, and races.
- Elementary meteorology and its effect on paddling conditions.

The youthful rivals must also exercise their ability among sunken cliffs and dashing surges, now driven between a double wave upon the rocks, now whirled completely round, or buried in the foam. In this rough school, initiated into these perilous gymnastics, they learn to bid defiance to the heaviest tempest, and to conduct their barks to land through the rage of contending elements. (Crantz, History of Greenland, p. 141.)

The Eskimo "Kayaks" were, of course, a great attraction to us strangers, and as soon as possible I possessed myself of one. The necessary balance in this narrow, crank little vessel is very difficult for a beginner to acquire. One feels as if he were swinging on a knife-edge, and it is very necessary, so to speak, to keep your hair parted well in the middle. Yet when one sees the Eskimo dancing like seabirds on the crests of the waves the whole performance seems simply child's play. As soon as my "Kayak" was ready I took it down to the shore. I found it no easy matter to force my legs and as much else of me as was necessary through the narrow opening into the place where I was to sit. This done, I was carefully pushed out into the water, but the feeling that seized me just as I left dry land was one of unspeakable insecurity. The little craft rocked first to one side then the other, and every moment promised an immediate capsize. It seemed to me a simple impossibility that I should ever learn to sit it, and I looked with despairing envy and desire at the Eskimo, who were of course out to enjoy the sight of Nalagak in a "Kayak," and were darting hither and thither over the water, and throwing their little spears about with as much ease and indifference as if they were sitting safe on the floor at home. But practice has a wonderful effect, and after one or two outings I began to feel tolerably comfortable. I got on better still when I had a pair of outriggers or supports made to help me. These are miniature "Kayaks," about two feet long, and are fastened on each side of the canoe, just behind the seat. They make things considerably easier for the uninitiated of course, but the Eskimo themselves rarely use them, and I myself abandoned them after a while. (Fridtjof Nansen, The First Crossing of Greenland, trans. Hubert Majendie Gepp [London: Longmans, Green, and Co., 1892], pp. 402–3.)

• Coastal and offshore navigation. The aspiring kayaker should be able to plan sea journeys using a nautical chart, tide tables, a *Tidal Stream Atlas,* a volume of the *Coastal Pilot* for the area, and if necessary a topographical map to plan suitable campsites.

At all times the proficient sea kayaker will carry spare paddles, flares, torch, compass, whistle or fog horn, a change of clothing, some emergency food (chocolate or candy bars), the means of making a hot drink, a first aid kit (including a polyethylene exposure bag), and a repair kit for the kayak and accessories.

All equipment should be serviceable and well maintained. All bags and containers must be completely watertight. In some parts of the world certain items of equipment will be dictated by local circumstances. Some examples would be firearms for protection against wild animals or local bandits, a bang stick for sharks, or a mosquito head net for the smaller varieties of wild beast.

With the necessary free time, a little determination, the correct equipment, good conditions in which to practice, and someone to offer guidance at the appropriate times, an individual can become proficient in handling a sea kayak in a couple of months or even weeks. Of course, complete competence is achieved only through experience. Unlike the case with novices in many other physical sports, it is rare for any enthusiastic novice sea kayaker to feel handicapped by mere years. Nor is it necessary for those over thirty, forty, or even over fifty years old to fade away from top level sea kayaking. It would appear that, with our sport, what one loses in youth and speed is often vastly outweighed by maturity, experience, and sheer exuberance.

Maneuvers

Beach Launch.   For the basic and simple beach launch (fig. 24A) place the kayak on the sand at the waterline and seat yourself with the paddle held upright in one hand. Then use your free hand to push the boat toward the water and at the same time hitch forward with your body until the kayak is afloat.

If there is any surf running, time your launch so it is made during a lull in the wave patterns. Large swells arrive near the coast in groups or sets of six to eight parallel waves. After a set, there is usually a lull

of several minutes when the waves diminish considerably. Once on the water, paddle quickly to clear the breaking surf. If a wave appears, take it head on and paddle straight through. Do not lift your arms above your head, but rather lean forward into the wave and keep the head down.

If the beach slopes steeply and there is a dumping surf (i.e., the waves crash down steeply without any run to the beach), it may be necessary to have someone hold your kayak steady at the water's edge and give you a shove during a lull in the waves. In these circumstances the last person off the beach should be the most experienced because there will be nobody to steady his kayak and push him off.

For all beach launchings in very cold conditions, it is advisable to use a small piece of driftwood to push yourself into the water. This will in most cases prevent the discomfort of beginning your paddle with a cold, wet hand.

Rock Launch.   For the rock launch (fig. 24B) lay your paddle across the rear of the cockpit to form a bridge between the kayak and a rock. Carefully balance with the paddle and sit down by placing your legs one at a time inside the boat. Be sure to lean slightly toward the rock to prevent a capsize seaward. When you are seated and have the spray cover in place, it may be necessary to take the weight off the kayak with the paddle and your free hand so that the kayak can float clear of any rocks that lie just below the surface.

24. Basic launching methods include: the beach launch (A), the rock launch (B), and the seal launch (C).

Seal Launch. Launching can be difficult in areas where rocks and cliffs are abundant with no flat beaches to be found, but with careful positioning and timing you can successfully launch in fairly rugged terrain. Figure 24C illustrates a seal launch down a rock covered with seaweed. For this launch you position the kayak at the top of the rock or at any place on it where you can balance the kayak for entry. Once seated, hold the paddle upright with one hand and push with the free hand to gain momentum. You must balance carefully as the boat slides down into the water.

Another kind of seal launch (not illustrated) can be attempted if there is a swell running and there are flat rocks available above the level of the water. Position your kayak and seat yourself in it at a point where the larger waves wash up over the higher rock slabs. It should be only a matter of minutes before a swell larger than the rest rises up to lift the kayak off the rock. With careful timing, you can help the water under the hull to float the kayak off the rock: holding your paddle in one hand, partially support the weight of the kayak on your paddle and free hand and at the same time hitch forward with your body.

Side Drop. The side drop launch (fig. 25) from the side of a jetty or a similar platform may be used (when all other methods prove impossible). It is a difficult maneuver and is for the advanced kayaker, but is well worth knowing. The side drop can be used when the kayak is four to five feet above water level.

25. The side drop is an emergency maneuver performed from a platform or jetty four to five feet above the water level.

With care it works just as well from greater heights as long as the launching platform and the landing place are clear of obstructions and the water is deep. The side drop can even be used if you have to launch from the side of a small boat. However, I have never tried this with a fully loaded kayak.

It is best practiced in a swimming pool, first from the side, then from a low springboard. The boat must be positioned with extreme care so it half rests on the platform and half hangs in space. As you enter the cockpit and prepare for the launch, all your weight must be kept toward the platform or the boat will overturn. Once seated, place the spray cover into position and give the kayak momentum by swinging the paddle forcefully across your body and slightly upward. At the same time jerk your body—with the kayak—upward and outward into space. During this takeoff it is important not to lean too far out because this could cause the kayak to hit the water on its side, and this in turn could cause a capsize. In any event, be prepared to execute a support stroke (high brace) as the kayak hits the water.

Basic Landing. Try to choose an area where the surf is small—at the sides of a bay rather than in the center of it or on a weather shore (a shore lying to the windward). If a surf is running, determine how close you can get to the shore and still remain outside the area where the largest waves are breaking. As with a launch, time your landing so it is made during a lull in wave patterns. Sit and observe the relation between the waves and the lulls. Choose a lull and paddle in on the back of one of the waves as it rolls in toward the beach (fig. 26). When you paddle on the back of a wave, you work directly against the water particles, which are traveling in the opposite direction (see fig. 34, p. 37). As a consequence, your forward progress is retarded, and you will be left behind to wallow in the trough of the wave. This, of course, will put you on the face of the next incoming wave. The danger now is that the boat will surge forward on the face of this new wave. To prevent this and to hold yourself back until the swell has passed, execute a few reverse paddle strokes. As the wave passes beneath you, paddle hard again on its back. You will begin to make headway toward the beach. It may be necessary to repeat this maneuver several times before the waves are small enough to be disregarded and the kayak is in shallow water.

In a group situation, the leader or another experi-

26. Landing in a small surf. (Photo by Alan Ainslie.)

enced paddler appointed by the leader chooses the path to shore and lands ahead of the main party. Once on the beach, this person can view the lines of surf as they approach, time the lulls, and then, using hand signals, direct each paddler into shore. The person on shore can be of particular help to novices who are often reluctant to turn their heads around in surf for fear of losing their balance.

Landing in a Dumping Surf. It is difficult and often dangerous to land in a dumping surf. These waves are caused by a bottom with a steep shelf. Each wave quickly reaches its critical depth and then peaks and breaks suddenly, dragging with it sand and small stones, which rise up inside the curl. The wave and stones crash down on the paddler with great impact. The breaking of a dumping wave is almost as explosive because the air that is trapped and compressed inside the curl exerts tremendous pressure.

In a dumping surf, you still must attempt to take advantage of the lulls between sets of waves. The waves in these lulls are smaller than the waves in the sets. They are, however, still dumping waves. Because of the characteristics of these waves, you must paddle frantically in order to maintain your position on

the back of the wave. Even when you are touching ground, you will need to use your paddle and hand to grab into the sand to prevent being sucked back into the next wave.

Again it is essential that an experienced paddler land first. Not only must he guide and reassure other paddlers as they come in, but he must grab their boats, drag them up into the sand, and hold them steady while they make a hasty exit.

In any kind of surf, it is advisable for inexperienced paddlers to land one at a time and to keep a good distance from one another. It is not necessary for everyone to dash for the same wave or even the same lull.

Seal Landing. The necessity of performing a seal landing (see fig. 27) depends on the prevailing conditions. If a landing is necessary and there is no convenient flat beach at hand, it becomes obvious that other plans have to be made. You must improvise and use whatever physical features are at hand. The type of rock you choose to land upon will depend upon the type of local rock formations, but flat rocks will of course give a much softer landing than the more jagged variety.

First select a potential landing spot over which the swell surges from time to time, and where a landing might be accomplished without any damage (fig. 27A). Time the frequency and height of the swells that cover the spot. When a large enough swell is about to wash over the landing place, paddle hard on the back of the swell, so that there is water covering the surface of rocks as the kayak arrives over the chosen spot (fig. 27B). The idea is to plant the kayak down gently as the water subsides and then jump out of the kayak quickly and pull it out of harm's way before any following swells surge up over the rock and wash the kayak off (fig. 27C). Like most advanced skills, the seal landing is best practiced in controlled conditions. Choose a time when the swells rise up gently over flat rocks that are protected by a good covering of weed. Success in conditions such as these will give you confidence to attempt a seal landing when the sea and the rocks are less inviting and the urgency is greater.

Strokes and Braces

Forward Stroke. A competent sea kayaker should be able to paddle at an average speed of three

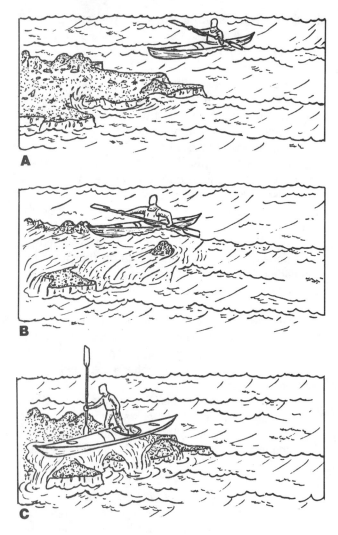

27. The seal landing enables a kayaker to land on rock formations.

to four knots. This is especially necessary if any sort of progress is to be made in adverse tidal streams. But to maintain a steady speed over many miles it is important to cultivate a good, productive, and economical style of paddling. A well-executed forward stroke will accomplish this.

Stretch the arm out and place the blade into the water well out in front of you, without making a splash. Curve the spine forward. The whole body will help pull the blade back but to do this you must swing the shoulders from the waist. The pushing hand does not cross over the center line of the kayak. As the right arm pulls back, the right foot will press on the

footrest and as the left arm pulls back, the left foot will press and so on. For a fast stroke in calm weather, keep the paddle blades close to the side of the kayak. In rough seas or high winds allow the paddle to sweep farther out to the side. With a straight-keeled sea kayak this should not affect the boat's directional stability to any extent. By slightly angling the upper edge of the submerged paddle toward the stern, you will find that the moving blade both gives support and propels you forward. If the wind and waves are on the beam or are quartering aft (i.e., coming from the stern and about forty-five degrees to the side), the tendency will be for the kayak to swing around (usually it will be the bow that will try and point into the wind). Novices tend to correct this by paddling harder on one side than the other. Over many miles this can be tiring and unpleasant. There is a better way.

Suppose the high wind is on your right side (starboard). Lean your boat over onto its right side. The curve of the hull's waterline is now in the position of a keel. This will cause the kayak to cut a slightly curved track through the water. To hold the boat in this position, brace your upper or left knee under the cockpit coaming and straighten the lower or right leg. The deck of the boat is now correctly presented to any waves breaking on the beam. This position can be maintained comfortably for many miles. To counteract any sudden swing around, you should sweep out as far as you can by straightening out your right arm. Increase the supporting angle of the blade and push yourself back on track by an extra vigorous sweep while leaning the kayak a little farther over. Practice this in calm water before trying it on the open sea.

Sweep Stroke. The sweep stroke is a simple way of turning a kayak or correcting direction when your kayak is not running straight.

To execute a sweep stroke reach well forward and place the paddle blade into the water close to the side of the hull with the driving face outward and the top edge of the blade angled slightly in the direction of the sweep. You should be braced firmly in the cockpit. Sweep the paddle outward and back with the whole blade submerged so that it travels in a semicircle. Allow the kayak to lean over toward the paddle, which is pushed out as far as possible from the side. The stroke will finish with the paddle near the stern. Because the kayak leans over onto the gunwale, it will turn much easier than if in an upright position. As the paddle nears the stern, allow the boat to come up-

28. The reverse sweep stroke.

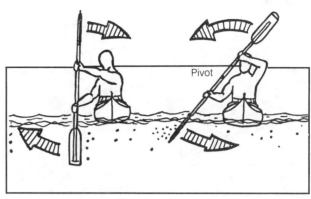

30. The draw stroke helps a kayaker position himself during rescues.

29. The forward sweep stroke.

right again. The kayak will be supported only so long as the angled blade is moving. In strong winds or rough seas, the paddle may be held in the extended position in order to gain better leverage.

To turn the kayak, execute a reverse sweep (fig. 28) on one side and a forward sweep (fig. 29) on the other. The paddle blade should be just below the surface, the arm reaching out fully extended and the elbow slightly bent. If the paddle blade is angled to give maximum support during the sweep, the kayak can be leaned well over, thus gaining an advantage from its width amidships and thereby giving the long

straight-keeled sea kayak a false rocker upon which to turn.

In beam seas created by high winds, it is sometimes easier to perform three or four strong reverse sweep strokes, leaning the boat and allowing the wind to help blow you around in order to start the boat moving. If the sweep stokes are timed carefully, the approaching waves can be used to pivot the boat thus making the turn much easier.

Draw Stroke. The draw stroke (fig. 30) is important for the quick positioning of boats during deepwater rescues and often vital during Eskimo rescues. It should be done with determination so that kayaks can be positioned regardless of any chop on the surface of the sea. Every second counts, especially with an Eskimo rescue, but it takes strength to move a long kayak sideways against a beam wind. On the other hand, if the stroke is helped by a high wind it is all too easy for the boat to overrun the paddle blade, which can cause a capsize.

To execute the draw stroke, extend the paddle out over the side in the direction you wish to move and fully submerge the blade. Pivoting somewhere near the center of the paddle shaft, pull the driving face of the paddle blade toward you with your lower arm and push the other blade away from you with your upper arm until the paddle is nearly vertical (fig. 30A). Then twist the shaft so the blades turn ninety degrees. Again pivoting near the center of the paddle shaft, push the submerged blade away from you with your lower arm and pull the upper blade toward you with your upper arm until the paddle is back to the starting position (fig. 30B). During the entire operation the lower blade should be submerged at a constant depth.

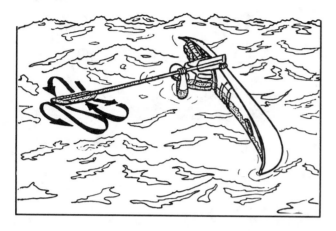

31. Sculling for support.

Sculling for Support Stroke. The sculling for support stroke will either hold you level with the surface of the water or scull you back into the upright position again. The stroke can be performed with the paddle held in either the normal or extended padding position. In figure 31 the paddler has capsized with a fully loaded reardeck. The air inside this equipment together with the buoyancy aid may prevent him from capsizing completely.

Move the paddle, which has been extended as shown in figure 31, to and fro in a small arc. During the movement, keep the leading edge of the blade high. At the point where the blade changes direction, raise the trailing edge of the blade to create a new leading edge. In this way the paddle planes just be-

32. The stern rudder is a steering stroke used to correct directional instability caused by a following sea.

low the surface and supports you or raises you into the upright position.

Stern Rudder. The stern rudder (fig. 32) is primarily a steering stroke, and its main application in sea kayaking is to correct any directional instability caused by a following sea, whether it is inshore surf or on the open ocean. A following sea (when the waves approach from the rear) can be difficult to handle because if the waves are large enough, the kayak will surf forward.

For this stroke place the paddle in the water vertically, about a foot out from the side toward the stern. The back of the blade faces outward. To apply the stroke, push the blade out and away from the side while the boat is moving forward. The boat will turn on that side.

There is a procedure for coping with a following sea so that energy can be used economically and the danger of a capsize minimized. After a kayak has been overtaken by a wave, it will be retarded in the trough. At this stage, ease off the forward paddle stroke and increase to full effort only when the next wave has caught up with the paddler and the kayak is again surging forward on the face of the wave (see fig. 34, p. 37). If you are inexperienced, this can be a little alarming. To combat any instability, the paddle shaft can be twisted so that the back of the blade is trailed almost flat on the surface of the water behind the paddler. If the boat tends to swing around away from the paddle stroke, you must change the paddle support over to that side quickly in order to have continued stability.

Paddle Brace. The paddle brace (fig. 33) is one of the most important of all sea kayaking techniques, and it is this technique that enables a paddler to remain upright while beaming onto a breaking wave. When you apply a paddle brace it is important that you fit snugly in the cockpit and are able to grip the underside of the cockpit coaming with your knees. If you are a slack fit, you will be plucked out of the cockpit and left bracing on the wave while the kayak goes bouncing to shore without you.

The paddle brace is used mainly for landing through surf, playing in surf, or running before steep following waves out on the open sea.

To execute the paddle brace on a large wave (fig. 33A) lean your kayak well over into the breaking wave, throwing your weight on the downward driving face of the paddle. You must place the paddle into the

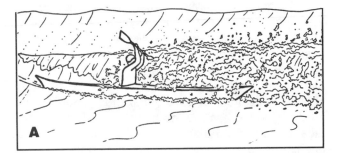

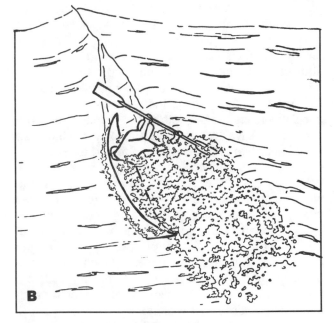

33. The paddle brace enables the kayaker to remain upright while beam onto a large (A) or small (B) breaking wave.

face of the toppling wave or as high as possible into the foam.

To execute the paddle brace on a small breaking wave (fig. 33B), place the paddle on top and just a little behind the wave with the driving face of the paddle downward. The blade will be supported on the upsurge of water inside the wave, but you must lean over into the oncoming wave to maintain the brace; if not, you will capsize with considerable violence in the direction the wave is traveling.

Handling Waves

Paddling over waves of one sort or another is what kayaking on the ocean is all about. Without waves the sport we love would be dreary and dull. It is waves, however, that cause novices many of their problems, so it is perhaps as well if we look at these sometimes perplexing water patterns.

Waves come in various shapes and sizes, ranging from mild ripples to what appear to be skyscraping nightmares. As you sit out on the open sea the first thing you will be aware of is the ground swell. I once heard this likened to a mouse crawling underneath a sheet. The sheet rises up as the lump passes beneath it, then the surface falls back into the same place again. This is what happens to the surface of the sea. As the swell passes and moves onward on its ponderous way to its ultimate destination, anything floating on the surface of the ocean will settle back again into almost the same position it was in before the swell passed beneath it. Because of this, the largest deep-water swell is quite harmless to the ocean paddler. Remember, however, that you may eventually have to land, and majestic, awe-inspiring swells can create frighteningly dangerous surf. Old swell patterns can be complicated by more recent swells coming from a different angle, or even from a different direction altogether.

To add to the confusion, a strong wind may whip up steep seas from yet another direction and reflected waves from a pier, breakwater, or cliff can confuse the pattern even further. The newcomer to ocean kayaking will probably find this all bewildering, and only experience will bring confidence.

Following Sea. To the experienced paddler on open waters, the following sea is a free ticket. As he surfs forward, covering many miles with ease, his only problem may be to avoid cutting into the side or ramming the rear end of the one of his companions. For the leader who tows a tired group member, the danger of a following sea is that the exhausted person may collide with or overrun the person towing.

A following sea causes the waves most feared by the inexperienced paddler, who would much rather be paddling into them. As the waves come from behind, they catch up with the unfortunate novice. The angle of his kayak tilts forward, he becomes unstable, and gets the impression—usually a correct one—that he is being thrown forward fast and is out of control. As the kayak is thrust forward, the wave will cause it to swing around and broach and this can all too easily cause a capsize. (For the remedy see discussion of the stern rudder fig. 32, p. 34.)

One day as we were out fishing in still, calm weather, the sky suddenly darkened to the south. We knew the wind was coming, and gathered up our lines with all haste. But before we were ready the storm was upon us, first with a few preparatory gusts, and then in all its wild fury. The sea flew black and white before it, the calm surface was soon one sheet of foam. The current and the wind met here; the green waves broke in crests of white spray, and the canoes were lost to each other in the hollows. We had to make for shore to save our fish and ourselves, and we paddled away as fast as we could go with the sea on our beam. . . .

. . . You have to keep a sharp eye on these big breaking seas, for if one of them catches the canoe before the paddle is well out on the leeside there is every chance of its occupant going to the bottom for ever and a day.

When we reached the shore we kept along it under shelter. Then we ran northwards fast before the wind, and now the "kayak" was even harder to manage than before. The big seas came rolling up from behind, and it was no easy matter to keep an even keel. As the wave comes you give a couple of powerful strokes and let the paddle float out to the side. Then the stern is lifted high in the air and you lean hard back. As the wave breaks you feel a heavy blow on the back, while the spray showers round you, and you seem to fly through space on the foaming crest. Then it rolls by you, you sink into the hollow, and with a few more vigorous strokes you ride again on the back of the next wave.

I had a good companion and instructor in Eliase, who kept the whole time as close to my side as the sea would let him. Now he would shoot past me on the top of one wave, and then I would ride by him on the next. It was a dance with the waves and a game with danger.

Presently the shore turned westwards and again offered us shelter. But first there was a belt of ice to pass, and it was necessary to bring the canoes through without getting them crushed between the moving floes. We found an opening and seized the opportunity, and with a few quick strokes sailed through on the top of the sea. (Nansen, The First Crossing of Greenland, *pp. 422–24.)*

Although a following sea can give an easy ride to the experienced paddler, it is easy to waste energy by attempting to paddle when your kayak is in the wrong position on the wave.

In Figure 34, the paddler feels the wave surge him forward (fig. 34A), and he increases the strength of his paddle stroke to get the maximum amount from its effect on his boat. As he moves quickly down the face of the wave, he executes a stern rudder on his left-hand side, thus keeping himself on track.

The wave passes beneath the paddler (fig. 34B) and he immediately feels the retarding effect of his position on the back of the wave crest. This is the time when he should ease off the strength of his stroke until the next swell catches up with him.

In the trough (fig. 34C), the paddler is almost standing still. As he feels the stern lift, however, he should increase the strength of his paddle stroke. The angle of his kayak will increase as the face of the wave rises under him and he will begin to surf forward.

If you are a novice and unsure of your balance, do not increase the strength of your paddle stroke when you feel your stern rise as in figure 34C. In this way, you will not allow your kayak to reach "surf velocity" (speed of the wave). If the waves are steep and perhaps—to your horror—curling over at the crest, take great care. As the stern of the kayak lifts to the wave, give a couple of reverse strokes to act as a brake and thus prevent the kayak from reaching surfing speed against your wishes.

Beam Sea.   These waves come from the side, giving novices the feeling that they are going to be bowled over sideways. In situations like this, lean gently into the waves and as you paddle forward, angle the top of your rearward traveling blade slightly toward the stern. In this way the blade is giving you support as well as propulsion. At the end of the stroke, when the paddle blade is at the rear and the driving face is almost tilted upward, you may find it necessary to support yourself. Do this by trailing the back of the blade along the surface of the water in the low brace position as a wave breaks over your gunwale.

Large breaking beam seas are best dealt with by employing a paddle brace. If a large wave catches you out and breaks over you, at the very moment when the paddle blade on that side is halfway through a forward paddle stroke, it may be necessary to flick the rear traveling blade over into the high brace support position (see fig. 33, p. 35).

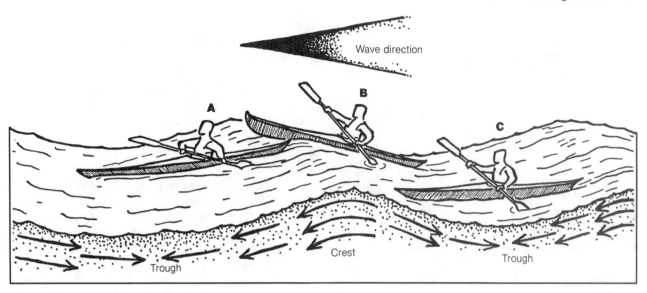

34. Conserving energy in a following sea.

Head Sea.   Paddling into oncoming seas on a moderately calm day is pleasant for novice and expert alike. The novice gets a feeling of stability, and even seasoned paddlers have the sensation of traveling over the water much faster than they really are. If, however, these approaching seas are caused by a high wind it often takes determination and strength to battle against them. Even though the waves may be small, the wind will drain your strength and, what is more important, your will and morale. Remember, keep calm and keep your head down. You will move forward slowly, even into the teeth of gale force winds.

When an ocean swell travels into shallow water, the bottom drag causes the wave to slow down. This means that the wave in deeper water will catch up. When this happens we say that the wavelength, or the distance between the wave crests, has become shorter. The nearer a wave gets to the shore, the steeper it becomes. The wave following behind is always in deeper water, but its distance to the wave in front is always getting shorter. Due to the decreased wavelength, the leading wave will become unstable, whereupon it will topple over and break.

A breaking wave can take two main forms. It can either plunge or spill.

Plunging, or Dumping, Waves.   These occur when an approaching swell meets a shore that is steeply sloping. All goes well until the wave reaches a point where its depth is about equal to its height. As

soon as that point is reached, the wave will overbalance forward, topple over, and break with an explosive release of energy, usually mingled with pebbles, sand, and grit, and sometimes even large logs! It is the crushing force of these dumping waves that causes kayakers so much concern during landings and launchings from steeply angled beaches (see p. 29).

Spilling Waves.   This is the kind of wave beloved of surfers. As the swell approaches a gently sloping beach, the wave will start to break gradually in water approximately twice as deep as it is high. At this point, the wave crest will tumble over and spill down the face of the wave. Because it lacks the violence of the dumper, this type of wave is quite manageable to anyone paddling inshore with a landing in mind—so long as the usual surf techniques are applied when appropriate (see p. 34–35 for Stern Rudder and Paddle Brace).

Refraction.   Waves sometimes bend when they begin to slow down upon reaching shallow water. This is known as refraction. In figure 35 the approaching waves are affected by the breakwater. The part of the wave closest to the obstacle will be the first affected by the shallow water. This will slow down that end of the wave. The effect is rather like that of a rank of marching soldiers turning a corner; the inside men march on the spot, while the outside men maintain their speed and pace and swing around. As the waves bend, they also lose height, so whereas the

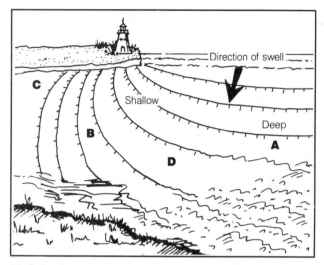

35. Refraction.

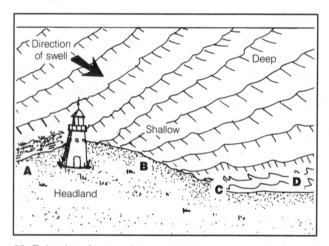

36. Refraction of waves along a shoreline.

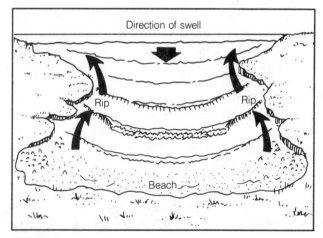

37. Refraction of swell in a small bay.

breaking waves at A are quite violent, those at B will be much more manageable, and a trouble-free landing could probably be made at C. The surf at D is getting increasingly larger and more intimidating.

Figure 36 shows the behavior of a swell traveling along a shoreline. The side of the headland at A is receiving the main force of the waves, making landings difficult in all but the calmest conditions. The best place for a landing will be at B where the shallow water causes the wave to refract and reduce in size. A landing at C might be possible, but coming ashore at D would be dangerous.

Bays usually provide good landing conditions and excellent places to go surfing. Figure 37 shows what happens when an ocean swell enters a small bay. The largest surf is in the middle, but because of refraction, the size of the waves diminishes toward the sides. Water is drained back out to sea by rips. These rips will also help flatten down the surf, making these areas good for a dry launching and an almost surf-free landing.

Refraction Round an Island. In figure 38 an ocean swell is approaching a small island or a rocky islet close inshore. The waves are influenced by the presence of the landmass, so they are refracted and bend around the island in the manner shown. Beyond the island the swells converge, and here standing waves of varying severity are formed.

Close to the island at A, the waves will be small. At position B the angle of the meeting waves may cause peaks to form in a manner similar to that illustrated in figure 40. Farther away from the island at C, the angle of approach is much more acute due to the refraction of the wave. It is in this area that clapotis may occur. When seeking shelter or a landing in the lee of an island therefore, this area should be approached with caution. Shallow water will increase the severity of any breaking seas.

Clapotis. In figure 39 the waves are striking the sea wall at a much more acute angle or perhaps even parallel to it. The wave is once again reflected, but instead of crossing the wave pattern at right angles, it rebounds and collides head on with the next oncoming wall of water. The result, which is frighteningly powerful and explosive, is known as clapotis.

This is not an area in which to play, unless you like living dangerously and the boat you are paddling belongs to someone else. I once sat only a few yards from a man who was attempting to see how close he

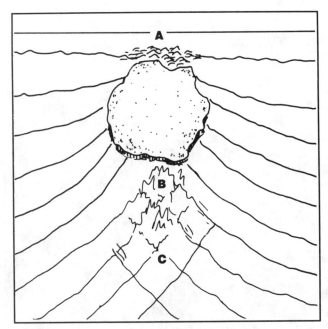

38. Wave refraction round an island. Some reflected waves may be caused at A. The danger spot is at B where the converging waves can cause "clapotis." The height of the waves act C will begin to decrease.

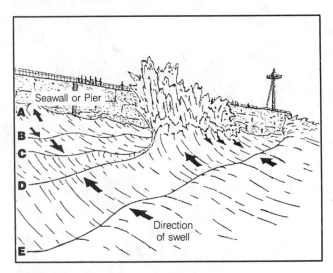

39. Clapotis.
A. Incoming swell surges up side of sea wall.
B. Huge amount of water falls back away from wall.
C. Returning swell speeds seaward.
D. Incoming swell collides with outgoing 'C.' This creates explosive 'clapotis,' sending water high into the air.

could get to the area of clapotis without getting wet. Unfortunately, due to a slight miscalculation on his part, to his horror and great fright, his world exploded

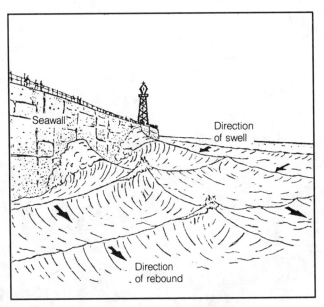

40. Reflection. Behavior of swell upon meeting an obstruction such as a sea wall or a vertical cliff.

beneath him. He proceeded skyward to a height of about twenty feet. The rescue was made in calm water only twenty yards or so from the danger area.

Reflection. In figure 40 the waves, generated by a swell, are approaching the sea wall at an angle only slightly less than ninety degrees. After coming into contact with the solid obstruction, the waves reflect off, converge, and are superimposed at right angles to the original wave pattern. When a crest meets a crest, the peak so formed will be higher than the original wave.

For the experienced kayaker, paddling in this rebound area can be an exhilarating experience. One moment the boat drops into a trough, the next it is picked up to pirouette on a pyramid of water. This is also an ideal area for advanced training. In the event of a capsize, however, and before a rescue is attempted, the swimmer should tow his boat and paddle out of the immediate vicinity of any breaking seas.

Even in the absence of any swell, I find that one of the most tiring seas is the short reflected chop caused by an onshore wind against a steep or rocky coastline. The small, bouncy reflected waves cause a kayak to twist about seemingly with a mind of its own. With boring monotony, every other stroke or so has to be accompanied by a corrective lean and sweep. Fortunately, the advent of drop-down skegs has helped to reduce this problem.

You cannot rank as an expert kaiak-man until you have mastered the art of righting yourself after capsizing. To do this, you seize one end of the paddle in your hand, and with the other hand grasp the shaft as near the middle as possible; then you place it along the side of the kaiak with its free end pointing forward towards the bow; and thereupon, pushing the end of the paddle sharply out to the side, and bending your body well forward towards the deck, you raise yourself by a strong circular sweep of the paddle. If you do not come right up, a second stroke may be necessary.

A thorough kaiak-man can also right himself without an oar by help of his throwing-stick, or even without it, by means of one arm. The height of accomplishment is reached when he does not even need to use the flat of his hand, but can clench it; and to show that he really does so, I have seen a man take a stone in his clenched hand before capsizing, and come up with it still in his grasp. (Nansen, Eskimo Life, pp. 52–53.)

THE ESKIMO ROLL
AND OTHER SELF–RESCUES

What was once a survival technique used by the Eskimo kayak hunters of the Arctic is now the normal way in which modern sea kayakers right themselves after an accidental capsize. Not everyone who paddles a kayak can Eskimo roll and not everyone wants to learn. It is, however, an easily mastered skill, especially if you are taught in the warm, pampering confines of a swimming pool by someone who knows what he is doing and can correct your mistakes while you are hanging upside down and worrying yourself to death.

Of all the different types of Eskimo rolls—and I teach ten methods to my students—I consider the screw roll the quickest and best in a survival situation. It can be performed without changing the hand position on the paddle, and because the paddle is not used in an extended manner as with some rolls, there is less chance of straining the shaft or snapping a blade.

Screw Roll

The screw roll is so called because while moving forward, the paddler appears to screw himself around and through the water without any break in the paddle stroke (see fig. 41).

If you think you are going to capsize, breathe in enough air to last you out and keep calm; a panicky paddler will not hold his breath for long. If the water is

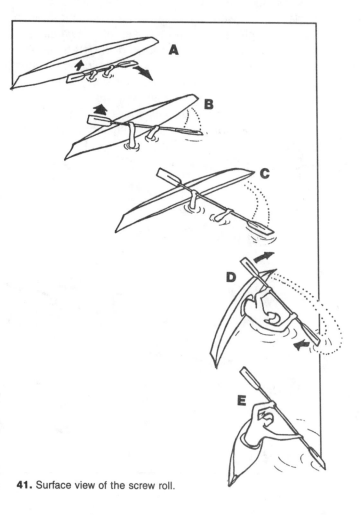

41. Surface view of the screw roll.

cold, be prepared for the shock of its icy fingers gripping your temples and taking your breath away.

As soon as you are upside down, you must get into the "wind up" (pronounced "wynd") or surface preparatory position for starting the roll (fig. 41A). Push your head and arms up toward the surface and the light. Assuming that you are right-handed, the angle of the oval paddle shaft, as you feel it in your left hand, will indicate to you the angle of the forward paddle blade (fig. 41B). (If you practice this on dry land with your eyes shut, it will help consolidate the movement and the hand positions in your mind.)

Push the right hand out from the side of the hull. At the same time, push the left hand up high enough to let the rear blade miss the hull of the upturned boat and allow the forward blade to sweep right around until it is at right angles to the kayak (fig. 41C and D).

If you hold the forward blade at the correct angle—that is with its leading edge high as it sweeps out—it will plane along the surface of the water, supporting you and lifting you toward the surface. The secret is to sweep out until your right biceps touches your nose. As it does so, jerk your right hand down violently, giving a small push upward with the left hand and simultaneously flick your hips (fig. 41E).

During the roll, the left foot should be pressing against the footrest and your knees should be spread apart so that they grip the underside of the cockpit coaming. If you do not do this, you will pull yourself right out of the kayak like a cork from a bottle. Some people find that leaning backward until their head almost touches the reardeck helps them roll more easily.

In figure 42 the paddler is sitting ready in the wind-up position. Throughout the roll, the hands must retain their normal paddling grip on the paddle. Consequently, when the wind-up position is adopted, the wrists must be bent down as far as possible. To fully appreciate the movement of the paddle during the roll, turn the book upside down and view the illustration in the inverted position.

Note: The front blade has its driving force upwards, while the outer and leading edge is angled slightly down toward the water. Once capsized, this paddle position will ensure that the outward sweep has a surface-planing action. It will also help if you twist your body through ninety degrees before pushing the head and arms up to the light, prior to the outward sweep.

Some people find it advantageous to practice the paddle movement standing on land without the kayak. The push up to the surface can be simulated by bending down at the waist. In this way, beginners can become used to the movements that their bodies and arms must perform, without the inhibiting effect of water up the nose.

During practice in warm, safe water, wear a

Fish Eye View

Surface View

42. Screw roll. Movement diagram.

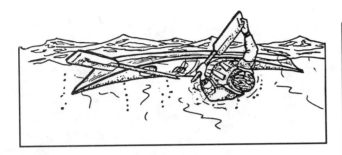

43. A broken paddle during an attempted roll.

noseclip. Hanging upside down with one half of your body in the water and the other half above water does your sinus cavities no good at all.

Do not let rolling a kayak full of equipment worry you. You will find that a fully loaded boat rolls just as easily as an empty one. The only time you will have a problem is if the reardeck has been used to carry a quantity of bulky equipment. You will find that the difficulty is not in rolling but in capsizing completely so that a 360-degree roll may be performed. This will depend to a large extent upon the amount of air trapped inside what you carry, which forces the kayak to lie on its side and stay there. If this happens, forget the roll, just scull up with the paddle on that side.

Remember, to master the Eskimo roll is a sign of success. To have to roll is a sign of failure. And, of course, just as you are about to break the surface, after what you consider to have been a textbook roll, your paddle shaft may snap.

Broken Paddle. In figure 43 the paddler had been attempting a Pawlata roll only to have the shaft of his paddle snap off completely.

Breaking a paddle in the act of rolling could be classified as one of life's little catastrophes. All is not lost, however, and you still might come through without having to swim. An Eskimo faced with the same problem would probably try to roll up using the throwing stick from his harpoon or even his knife. You will not have a throwing stick, but you should have one half of the paddle left in your hand. Do not panic and drop it.

Here is what you do (see fig. 44): Keep calm. Wrap your right hand around the edge of the paddle blade near the center (fig. 44A). Lean back so that your head is touching the reardeck. Hold the blade so that your palm is facing outward and your knuckles are against your left ear. Extend your left arm out at right angle to the boat, palm down, fingers slightly apart but

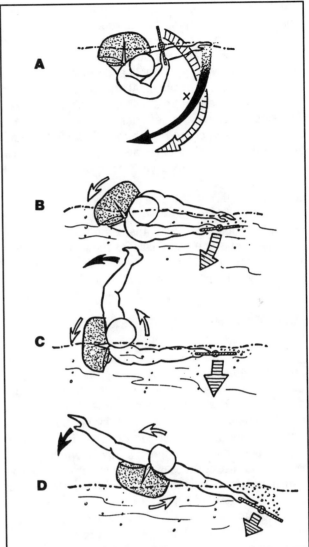

44. Recovering after breaking a paddle while rolling.

not fully open. Twist your head up toward the light on that (left) side. Strike down violently with your left hand, keeping the arm straight as it approaches position X (that is the limit of the left hand's effectiveness). Your right hand will now follow the path of the left hand by striking out and down with the paddle blade.

As the blade on its downward sweep passes the left hand (fig. 44B), throw the left hand over violently (fig. 44C) in the direction of the solid arrow. This acts as a counterbalance and helps the kayak to flick over (fig. 44D) and complete the roll.

Throughout this whole maneuver, *your head must remain touching the reardeck. If your head comes off you won't come up.* To practice the amount of sweep needed and the sequence of left and right hands, stand with your back and head touching a wall, your arms in position. At the start of the right-hand sweep, the fingertips will be touching the wall, knuckles touching the left ear. At the end of the sweep, the palm of the right hand will be flat against the wall on the right side. Remember, when you are in the kayak you must keep your head on the reardeck while twisting your hips and body in the direction opposite to the thrust of the paddle blade.

If you wish to take this maneuver even further, gradually reduce the size of the blade area held in the right hand and you will finish up performing a hand roll. To gain extra surface pressure from your hand alone, open the fingers slightly.

Headstand

Although the headstand was first publicized in Germany more than forty years ago as part of some rolling instructions, it is not strictly speaking a roll but more a support stroke: you go over and come up on the same side. Unlike the sculling for support stroke, the headstand is one that can be done from a completely inverted position and is for those whose rolling capabilities are perhaps a little suspect or who find themselves lying on the surface of the water with a fully loaded reardeck. This is especially so for those who find themselves capsized on their "wrong" rolling side (i.e., on their left side if they are right-handed or on their right side if they are left-handed).

Figure 45 shows how to capsize on the right-hand side. As you capsize, let the right blade slice down, bringing the left one over. While this is happening, change your hand position (fig. 45A). Let go of the shaft with your left hand and grasp the lower blade, fingers outward. Turn your right hand over on the paddle shaft so that your palm is facing outward (fig. 45B). Once you are completely upside down, twist your body sideways and allow your chest and shoulders to rise parallel to the surface of the water. If you are in clear, shallow water, the bottom should be directly facing you. Place the paddle shaft over your right shoulder so that the blade is sticking straight up into fresh air. The palm of your right hand is still facing outward. To raise yourself to the surface, strike

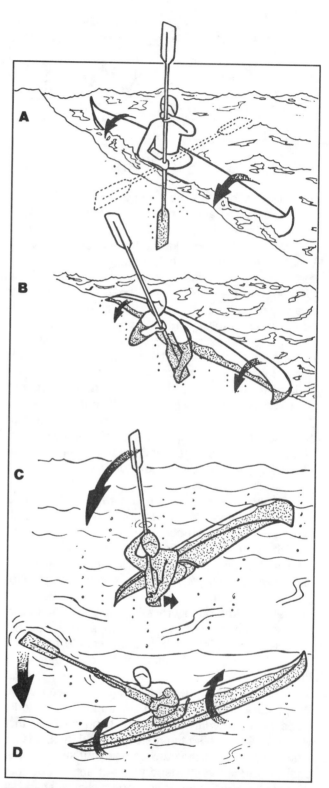

45. The headstand can be done in place of a roll when capsizing.

the paddle down violently with your right hand (fig. 45C). As the extended paddle strikes the water, lift the near blade with your left hand. As your body breaks the surface, flick your hips (fig. 45D).

Paddling Alone

Paddling alone on the sea is dangerous, but if you must, take certain precautions:
- You should be able to do an Eskimo roll on the first try.
- You should be suitably dressed for immersion.
- You should fit your kayak with either watertight hatches, bulkheads, and a bilge pump; a pod; or flotation material or inflatable buoyancy that fills the boat fore and aft to capacity and is securely fixed in position and tailored to the shape of the kayak. A plastic cup or bailer should be attached to a string.
- You should use a paddle leash in difficult conditions.
- You should take normal safety precautions (flares, personal buoyancy, notifying the Coast Guard of your plans).
- You should perfect a method of self-rescue in the event that a roll is unsuccessful.

Self-Rescues

In the event of a capsize, the first thing to do is remove yourself from the conditions that capsized you. If it is inside the surf line and it is too dangerous to swim in, tow your kayak well outside the area. Swimming at right angles to an overfall or tide race should get you out of it and into water that is a little calmer.

Reentry and Roll. The reentry and roll is an unassisted self-rescue for the lone paddler who for some reason finds himself in the water, out of his kayak, and alone.

Position the kayak so that the bow is pointing toward any oncoming waves. Face the stern and hold both sides of the cockpit coaming (fig. 46A). Hold the paddle on the side you are used to for rolling. If you have been paddling alone, you should be wearing a paddle leash. Relax and take a deep breath. Throw your head backward and down and bring your legs up and into the cockpit (fig. 46B). In a practice session

when you are not wearing a buoyancy aid, you will find that you finish up in the seat after a simple, underwater back somersault. However, a buoyancy aid will float you up on one side during reentry, and this could confuse you. You must maintain a firm grip on the cockpit coaming so the kayak maintains its position in relation to you as you enter. Roll up. If you are without bulkheads, hatches, or a pump, balance carefully and replace the spray cover. Open the waist elastic to gain access to the cockpit area, then start bailing. Support yourself by placing the paddle across the shoulder and sculling. This is hard work, but the larger the bailer the less time it takes.

If you are carrying a paddle float, you could put it on the end of the paddle to give support, as an alternative to sculling.

With bulkheads, hatches, and pump, balance carefully, replace the spray cover, and start pumping. You may have to rest the paddle across your shoulders and scull for support (fig. 47). If your kayak is fitted with a pod—or a device that acts in a similar manner—you need to paddle into calmer water, mop out whatever little water has entered your cockpit area, and then replace your spray cover.

In rough seas, the spray cover must be in place

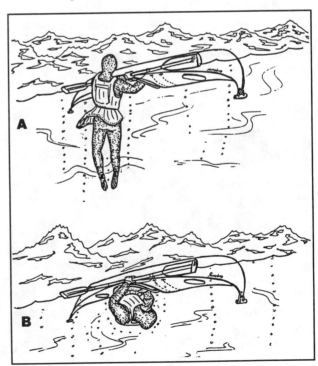

46. The reentry and roll is an unassisted self-rescue.

47. Sculling for support while pumping.

before emptying starts, otherwise the kayak will fill up again as fast as you get the water out. The spray cover must be large enough around the waist to allow the paddler to bail through it. This adaptation to the cover is one you may have to do yourself. You must be able to get the bailer down between your knees if you hope to get any water out, so don't make the bailer too large.

Paddle Float. Novices should not paddle out into open water alone. However, when the water is smooth and unruffled, and the air is warm, the temptation can be irresistible, and people will go out unaccompanied despite advice to the contrary.

48. The paddle float. (Photo by Will Nordby.)

The novice who capsizes will probably not attempt an Eskimo roll. An underwater reentry will not be part of his repertoire. In a book of this nature, I feel there should be a description of at least one solo rescue that a frightened novice can attempt with a reasonable chance of success.

The paddle float is not meant for rough seas, and although I have seen experienced kayakers succeed in rough conditions, this was due more to their experience and perseverance. This rescue is for the unpracticed paddler who is overbalanced by a gust of wind or capsizes for some other reason on calm water.

The method originated in Europe. When it was first described, however, it was not taken seriously by sea paddlers. In this method, some means of portable flotation is fastened to the end of the paddle, which is then used as an outrigger. The original suggestion, that one's life jacket should be removed and secured to the end of the paddle, was greeted with only a small amount of enthusiasm. However, because reentry can be performed by a lone paddler, it was not completely discarded.

The method was refined on the West Coast of the United States by substituting a plastic water container for the life jacket. Thus, removing one's protection was no longer necessary. Unfortunately, the novice still had to fiddle with knots in order to tie the float to the paddle, which is not the sort of exercise that a frightened novice needs. The system was improved further by Will Nordby of California. After a frightening capsize, he experimented with various air-filled floats and cushions to see if it was possible to make the paddle float easier to use. He and his friend Bob Licht of Sea Trek got together to design and market the first "paddle float."

This paddle float is simply a soft, strong plastic bag, and because the walls of the bag have an inner and outer skin, they can be orally inflated (fig. 48). The paddle float takes up little room, and for safety's sake it can be carried in a pocket on the life jacket. Once the float is slid over the end of the paddle blade and inflated, it cannot be removed until the air is let out again.

Before attempting to use the paddle float, make sure you have strong shock cord elastics fitted in a position that suits you (either on the fore- or reardeck) so that the paddle is held firmly in place.

In the event of a capsize, bail out and quickly right the kayak. Push the paddle through the deck

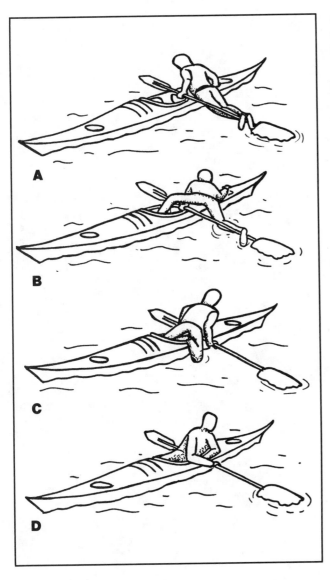

A

B

C

D

49. A self-rescue with a paddle float is an easy way for a novice to reenter the boat in calm water.

elastics *before* you fit the paddle float. Position yourself on the downwind side of the boat while inflating the float so that you do not lose contact with your kayak. Twist the outer paddle blade so that it lies flat on the surface of the water. Hoist your body up and onto the reardeck and hook your foot over the paddle (fig. 49A). Keep your weight on the float side and place the leading foot into the cockpit (fig. 49B). At the same time, shift the trailing foot onto the loom. Then move the trailing foot into the cockpit and slide both legs toward the bow (fig. 49C). Rotate your body forward while keeping your weight toward the float side (fig. 49D).

My advice to any frightened beginner who feels incapable of tackling this procedure is to spend time learning the Eskimo roll or cultivating a faithful companion.

DEEP-WATER RESCUES

Once you have decided that you are going to paddle a kayak, whether on the ocean, a lake, or a river, you may as well resign yourself to the fact that during the early learning stages, a few capsizes are to be expected. When you get better and more experienced, you become more adventurous and more willing to paddle in rough conditions, so there is always a chance of inadvertently becoming a swimmer. The best remedy for a capsize is undoubtedly the Eskimo roll. However, not everyone can or wants to Eskimo roll, and some kayaks are almost impossible to roll due to excessive beam or an inhibiting deck design. To overcome these problems, various methods have been developed over the years for emptying capsized kayaks and then putting the owners safely back into them. The water does not have to be very deep to merit this type of emergency procedure; in fact, water up to the eyeballs is just about right for a deep-water rescue.

Since I began kayaking on the sea, I have watched with humor, and sometimes horror, many rescue methods tried with varying degrees of success. I have observed group rescues with as many as six people working out a complicated rescue sequence involving an ingenious system of levers and pulleys brought about by the careful positioning of kayaks and paddles. I have observed solo rescues with a purple-faced man desperately trying to tread water in a rough sea while, at the same time, blowing down a large U-shaped tube inserted into his inverted cockpit, all in an effort to expel the water and raise the kayak. Needless to say, neither of these methods achieved widespread popularity.

The methods of rescue and reentry that follow should all be practiced in the calm waters of a sheltered bay or a swimming pool. It can be dangerous to practice under very cold or rough conditions.

Remember that it is vital that a capsized paddler maintain a firm hold on the kayak at all times, even if this means doing so during the bailout underwater. It is good to remember that even though initial practices may be on placid water where the upturned kayak stays in one place, in an open-water situation things might be very different, and the upturned kayak could be blown away faster than the capsized kayaker can swim after it. If your paddle drifts away during a rescue, always swim the kayak to the paddle. In windy weather, *never leave the kayak in order to swim to the paddle.*

After a rescue practice, the surface of the sea should not be littered with floating debris such as flare containers, lunch box, the contents of first aid and repair kits, or pieces of bloodstained polyethylene flotation foam.

As you become more proficient by all means progress to rougher water, but remember that it is *always* dangerous to perform any deep-water rescue inshore to breaking surf. In this sort of situation it is far safer to tow both man and kayak out of the danger area, whether it is amidst waves breaking against rocks or in a tidal overfall. Rough-water practice is always made safer by wearing crash helmets.

Group leaders will soon find that one capsize can be infectious. Others follow suit and attention may be divided between two or more calamities. Rescuers may have to neglect one of the rescues and

. . . A kaiak-man who has entirely mastered the art of righting himself can defy almost any weather. If he is capsized, he is on even keel again in a moment, and can play like a sea-bird with the waves, and cut right through them. If the sea is very heavy, he lays the broadside of his kaiak to it, holds the paddle flat out on the windward side, pressing it against the deck, bends forward, and lets the wave roll over him; or else he throws himself on his side towards it, resting on his flat paddle, and rights himself again when it has passed. The prettiest feat of seamanship I have ever heard of is that to which some fishers, I am told, have recourse among overwhelming rollers. As the sea curls down over them they voluntarily capsize, receive it on the bottom of the kaiak, and when it has passed right themselves again. I think it would be difficult to name a more intrepid method of dealing with a heavy sea. (Nansen, Eskimo Life, p. 54.)

thus lose the sense of urgency so important for getting people out of cold water or dangerous conditions as quickly as possible. Leaders may often find it necessary to use a combination of rescue techniques to solve difficult rescue situations or may invent some of their own.

The key to success is plenty of practice against the clock in controlled, choppy situations. For example, an HI rescue (see below) can be completed in fifty to sixty seconds, but only after a lot of practice.

HI Rescue

The HI rescue is so-called because of the position adopted by the kayaks on the water (see fig. 50). In this rescue, the person who has capsized and is in the water is rescued by two companions. Paddlers A and C position their boats quickly, collect paddler B's paddle, and then raft up facing him. Paddler B guides the bow of his upturned kayak between the two rescue craft. Paddlers A and C now lift paddler B's kayak up and over the paddles as quickly as possible (fig. 50A). This is really more of a snatch than a lift, thus allowing only a small amount of water to enter the boat. It is worth taking care to insure that the cockpit is clear of the water before starting to pull the kayak over the paddles. If paddlers A and C are careful, they will not damage the paddle shafts as they lift the boat over. The upturned kayak now rests and pivots on the paddles. Paddlers A and C hold the boat steady. As paddler B seesaws his end of the kayak up and down, the water drains out (fig. 50B). As soon as the boat is empty, the two rescuers turn it over into its upright position, slide it forward off the paddles, and pull the boat back between their two kayaks. The kayak is now in a position for paddler B to reenter by one of the methods discussed later (see p. 53).

With practice, this rescue should be completed in under a minute. As mentioned previously, at no time should the paddler in the water lose contact with the two rescue crafts. In high winds, it is possible that the two rescuers and the upturned boat will be blown away faster than the man in the water can swim after them.

TX Rescue

If you choose to paddle with only one other companion, you will need to know the TX rescue (fig. 51).

50. Lifting (A) and emptying (B) a capsized kayak during an HI rescue.

51. Lifting (A) and emptying (B) a capsized kayak during a TX rescue.

Because this can be completed successfully by only one other person, it is ideal for leaders and those in charge of inexperienced groups.

Paddler B snatches up the bow of the kayak as quickly as possible so as not to drag water into the cockpit of the capsized kayak. He then lifts the kayak across the foredeck of his own boat and pulls it until the cockpit rests near his own cockpit (fig. 51A).

Paddler B seesaws the kayak by leaning his own boat from side to side. Paddler A helps paddler B to control the emptying movement by holding onto the bow (fig. 51B). Once the boat is empty, it is turned right side up and paddler A reenters.

Paddler B must be especially careful before starting the seesawing operation. If there is too much water in the boat to be emptied, the excess weight will crack one or both of the decks. It might be prudent to remove the worst of the water by the curl method (see fig. 53, p. 53) before attempting the TX.

It is also easy for paddler B to damage his spray cover as he tries to drag the partially waterlogged kayak across his own cockpit. A good idea is to wear two spray covers. Wear the oldest and most repaired one underneath and remove the top one before the rescue starts. It is important that B looks after both pairs of paddles; this is when a paddle park (see p. 13) is useful.

It is possible for two boats to raft up and empty a third, in what then becomes a rafted TX rescue, but I do not consider it as efficient as the HI rescue. The HI and TX rescues have only limited success if the kayak is fully loaded.

Cleopatra's Needle

A frightening situation called Cleopatra's Needle develops when a kayak, with either too little buoyancy or badly distributed buoyancy, becomes swamped (fig. 52). If all the necessary precautions are taken before the trip starts, this will not happen; but it could happen to other groups that you may stumble across during the course of a gentle day's outing. On two occasions I have been able to assist complete strangers in the middle of large lakes, who have had only the point of their bows showing above the surface of the water. Not a pretty sight, but if you meet up with this it will be up to you to tell the man in the water how to empty his boat.

52. Cleopatra's Needle occurs when a kayak with incorrect buoyancy swamps.

In the past, any method of emptying a swamped kayak was very difficult, especially for frightened people of limited strength and experience. Some research was needed and, after a great deal of experimentation, I finally arrived at a method that seems to work every time and does not require an enormous amount of energy by the person in the water. I call this method the curl.

Curl

First, maneuver the kayak to the surface. This can be done by hooking the foot under the cockpit or diving down and grabbing the coaming and lifting up. Once the boat is lying on the surface with its cockpit uppermost, the emptying can begin (see fig. 53). The swamped boat lies alongside paddler B's. Its deck is completely awash. Paddler A pulls himself over paddler B's foredeck as near as he can to paddler B's cockpit, without getting in the way of B's paddle, and hooks his hands under the cockpit coaming of the swamped boat, his palms uppermost.

Paddler A rests his elbows on paddler B's deck, pulls the swamped kayak toward him, and tilts the cockpit so that the water starts to drain out (fig. 53A). Once paddler A's elbows are jammed against the deck by the weight of his kayak, B can then increase the draining angle by leaning over and sculling for support (fig. 53B). Apart from making sure that the

53. The curl is a method of emptying a swamped kayak.

draining kayak is held firmly and perfectly level, no further effort is required on the part of A. The aim of the rescue is not to empty the kayak completely, but to remove enough water so that the boat can be handled while performing one of the rescue methods previously described.

This method of rescue does not require exceptional strength. As long as paddler A can get his kayak on its side and hold it level, the water will drain out as paddler B controls the angle of the lean.

Methods of Reentry

Figure 54A shows a good, safe method of reentry: the paddles are made secure as a bundle across the two outside boats, and paddlers A and C have firm hold on the cockpit coaming of the inside kayak. Paddler B does not have to use a great deal of energy to get back into his kayak again, although he may feel a little undignified.

Figure 54B shows probably the best method of reentry involving only two people. Paddler A has one arm under the paddle shaft and is gripping the coaming with both hands. This will keep the raft stable, and as paddler B exerts his weight down onto the paddle, it will increase the stability. If padder B needs help, A can quite easily take his left hand off the cockpit coaming and grasp B's life jacket without losing stability.

54. Safe methods of reentry with two and three kayakers.

All-In Rescue

Weather conditions sufficient to capsize all three members of a kayaking group at the same time are bound to be absolutely horrific. Yet such weather conditions can come and go quickly. I know of at least one incident off the south coast of England in which a party of nine were hit by a bad squall. All capsized in the freak wind and came out of their boats. The storm passed as quickly as it came, but by the time a helicopter had arrived to rescue them, a number were suffering from exposure.

The all-in rescue will usually work even if all the paddlers of a group have been capsized. It is based on the principle that an upturned kayak can be used to form the pivot over which to empty another. To insure success, it is essential to practice the rescue in calm, sheltered waters or a swimming pool.

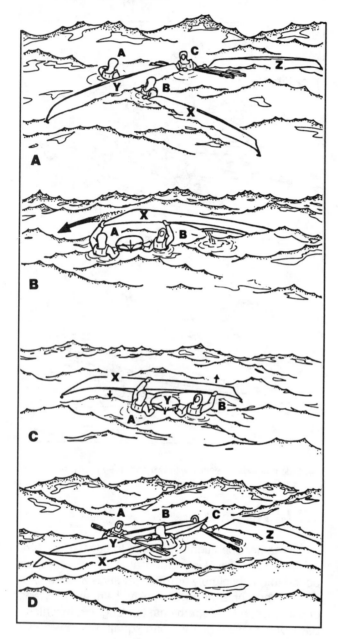

55. Emptying and reentering a kayak in the all-in rescue.

the paddles between his legs to free his arms. *On no account must he become separated from the main rescue.* Paddlers A and B hold on to the upturned cockpit coaming of kayak Y and face in opposite directions (fig. 55A). Paddler B lifts the bow of kayak X as high and as quickly as he can, so that the cockpit clears the water. As B does this he will automatically pull down on his right hand. However, any tilting of pivot boat Y is counteracted by A, who is holding on to the other side of the coaming. The less buoyant flotation contained by pivot boat Y, the more important it is for both men to hold it perfectly level and still; otherwise the air inside will escape and the boat will sink.

Paddler B passes kayak X over the pivot boat Y to A who continues taking it across until its cockpit rests on the upturned hull (fig. 55B).

Paddlers A and B seesaw kayak X until it is empty (fig. 55C). Once this is done, it is turned onto its right side and placed alongside the pivot boat. Paddler B positions himself next to his cockpit to get in first.

The reentry can be tricky in rough seas. Paddler B passes his paddle across the middle of pivot kayak Y (fig. 55D). To gain entry, B places his right hand at the rear of the cockpit of kayak X and in the center, while holding the paddle and the front of the cockpit coaming with his left hand. He enters the cockpit by kicking out with his feet and pushing down with his weight upon his arms. To counteract any unsteadiness caused by B's reentry, A pulls down on his end of the paddle shaft. As soon as B is secure in his boat, A's kayak can be emptied using the TX rescue, and C is finally put back in his kayak using the HI method.

The order of leaving the water is very important, and the leader has some decisions to make before the rescue commences. The most scantily dressed should hardly be the last one to leave the water, but if that person is already suffering from hypothermia and is put into his boat first, he might not be able to undertake the TX rescue.

During practice, the participants should change about, so that each person becomes familiar with every part of the rescue.

Eskimo Rescues

The Eskimo rescue is based on the assistance often given by one kayak hunter to another, mainly in

Figure 55 shows the beginning of a rescue and reentry involving three people. The sequence of the rescue can be applied to any number of paddlers. Paddlers A and B will perform the main rescue with kayak X. Kayak Y will serve as the pivot.

Paddler C holds on to his kayak Z and to kayak Y and looks after the paddles. If he wishes he can hold

Here comes a gigantic roller—they can see it shining black and white in the far distance. It towers aloft so high that the sky is almost hidden. In a moment they have stuck their paddles under the thongs on the windward side and bent their bodies forward so that the crest of the wave breaks upon their backs. For a second almost everything has disappeared; those who are further a-lee await their turn in anxiety; then the billow passes, and once more the kaiaks skim forward as before. But such a sea does not come singly; the next will be worse. They hold their paddles flat to the deck and projecting to windward, bend their bodies forward, and at the moment when the white cataract thunders down upon them they hurl themselves into its very jaws, thus somewhat breaking its force. For a moment they have again disappeared—then one kaiak comes up on even keel, and presently another appears bottom upwards. It is Pedersuak (i.e. the Big Peter) who has capsized. His comrade speeds to his side, but at the same moment the third wave breaks over them and he must look out for himself. It is too late—the two kaiaks lie heaving bottom upwards. The second manages to right himself, and his first thought is for his comrade, to whose assistance he once more hastens. He runs his kaiak alongside of the other, lays his paddle across both, bends down so that he gets hold under the water of his comrade's arm, and with a jerk drags him up upon his side, so that he too can get hold of the paddle and in an instant raise himself upon even keel. The water-tight jacket has come a little loose from the ring on one side and some water has got in; not much, however, but he can still keep afloat. The others have in the meantime come up; they get hold of the lost paddle, and all can again push forward. (Nansen, Eskimo Life, pp. 67–68.)

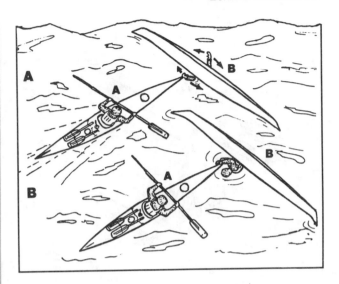

56. The bow rescue.

the Greenland area. Along these coasts it was often a practice for the paddler to lace the hem of his anorak to the wooden hoop of the cockpit coaming. This made the kayak thoroughly watertight, but it also made a quick exit impossible. In the event of a capsize and failure to roll, the unfortunate occupant had to rely on his nearest companion for assistance.

Briefly, the Eskimo rescue involves a method in which the paddler who capsizes remains in his kayak while a fellow paddler maneuvers his kayak to the upturned hull. The capsized paddler then rights himself by using any part of the rescuer's kayak or paddle that is offered.

Bow Rescue. Victim B keeps calm and bangs hard and quickly on his upturned hull to attract attention. Paddler B then raises his hands high in the air above the bottom of his hull and moves them slowly backward and forward. This makes it easier for A to place the bow of the rescue boat into B's hands (fig. 56A).

Once A sees that B has a firm hold on the lifting toggle (or his hands clasped tightly on the bow itself), he should paddle forward gently so that the rescued kayak is held steady against B's outward push as he raises himself to the surface (fig. 56B).

Paddler A must paddle into the rescue at a controlled speed. Remember that B, who is submerged, could be getting nervous and may decide to surface just at the very moment that A paddles in at break-

57. The Eskimo side rescue.

neck speed. Nobody wants a kayak up his nose at five knots. Paddler B should leave himself enough air so that if he feels he can wait no longer, he can make a calm, controlled exit. As he nears the surface, he should raise his hands above his head to warn the oncoming rescuer and to protect himself.

Side Rescue.   In the side rescue, the rescuer places his kayak parallel to the victim's kayak and offers his paddle to help the victim right himself (fig. 57A). This paddle forms a bridge across the two kayaks, providing a support that the upturned paddler cannot dislodge or push away during the act of pulling up to the surface (fig. 57B). This is by far the safest method of Eskimo rescue. Paddler A's kayak can approach the victim from any direction. The rescuer paddles either backward, forward, or sideways by means of a draw stroke. In some cases, it might even be more prudent for a rescuer who is approaching for a bow rescue to turn off at the last moment and perform a side rescue instead of risking injury.

It is important that A place his paddle well across the upturned hull. At the same time he places the victim's nearest hand onto the paddle shaft. While he waits for A to place his hands on the shaft the victim must control his anxiety and refrain from putting a vicelike grip on the first thing that his hand touches. If he grips the part of the paddle shaft on the opposite

side to the rescuer, he could foul up the rescue, prolong the time that he has to spend underwater, and cause a distressingly hysterical scene.

The moment B feels his hand placed onto A's paddle shaft he should pull himself to the surface using both hands. As the kayak turns toward the surface, B may find it necessary to change his hand position.

During the moment of capsize, B may notice that A is parallel to him but is downwind some distance away. This means that the speed of the rescuer's draw stroke will be slow. Paddler B can help things considerably by swimming his kayak toward the rescuer.

Swimming with the Kayak

The ability to swim with a kayak is an excellent survival exercise. If a paddle is lost during a capsize, it can be retrieved without leaving the cockpit. A capsized victim can assist in a practical way during Eskimo rescues by, if necessary, swimming his boat nearer to the rescuing kayak. The methods of swimming vary. Some people prefer to use a dog paddle, others use a kind of breaststroke. I prefer to use the method in figure 58. The right arm does a crawl stroke, while the other arm performs a powerful dog paddle and never breaks the surface. Some people find it difficult to raise their heads high enough to breathe and are, therefore, limited in the distance they can travel. Others appear to have no such problems and can swim indefinitely.

58. Swimming with the kayak to retrieve a paddle.

59. Swimming with the paddle.

Paddle Swimming

As well as being a good swimming pool exercise, paddle swimming has its survival applications, such as retrieving paddles during rescues. Quite fast speeds can be attained, but the secret is to roll the paddle blade forward on each stroke. The paddle blade is presented flat to the surface of the water and the downward push makes breathing easy by lifting the head out of the water. In figure 59, the driving faces are crosshatched and the back of the blade clear.

Factors Affecting Rescues

The success of all the rescues I have illustrated depends very much on a number of factors:

- The age and physical condition of the participants.
- Their level of fear and their general morale.
- The type of personal buoyancy and the clothing they are wearing.
- The distance between the group members at the time of the capsize.
- The skill level of the group and the speed with which they can maneuver.
- The condition of the sea and the strength of the wind.
- The distance from shore and the proximity of rocks.
- The temperature of the water.
- The weight of the equipment inside the upturned boat.
- The amount of equipment carried on the deck and how secure it is.
- The time of day and the presence or absence of fog.
- The prevalence of shipping.
- The amount of buoyancy inside the kayaks.
- The personal qualities and experience of the leader.

If a member of your group capsizes accidentally and the group consists mostly of novices, something has gone wrong with your plans. Either you have bitten off more than they can chew or the weather and tide have changed to the extent that the paddle is no longer a safe proposition, and you should start to think of the quickest and safest way back to sheltered water.

A Last Word on Rescues

It has to be acknowledged that there comes a time when the conditions take on a severity that makes any deep-water rescue quite impossible. Even putting oneself close to a swimming kayaker and his boat may place the rescuer in danger of having a man and an upturned kayak planted firmly on his head, followed closely by a dumping deep-water wave. In such a case, the only solution is to send out a distress signal and keep the patient in sight until help arrives.

SPECIAL PROBLEMS AFLOAT

Repairs Afloat

Kayaks can develop leaks on the open sea from a variety of causes. A collision while paddling too close to others in a following sea is a frequent cause. Sometimes a fault in manufacture can cause the same thing to happen in a less obvious manner. Careless launching is also a cause. I remember once paddling three miles out at sea in a kayak that I thought had its rear compartment filled with bricks. The expla-

nation was simple: it was full of water. During the launch from a sandy beach, the boat had rested on the upturned base of a broken bottle, producing several holes of varying size.

Whatever the cause of the damage, something must be done immediately. The victim should come alongside the rescuer, but face in the opposite direction. The victim then places his paddle behind his back and across the two boats. In that way he can steady it with both hands while he sits on it and proceeds to change boats. Once the victim is astride the rescuer's boat, the damaged kayak is lifted across the foredeck (fig. 60).

Nervous victims may feel safer sitting astride the reardeck so that they can hang onto the man in the rescuing craft. The boat to be repaired, however, forms an outrigger and stabilizes both boats so that it is just as easy for the victim to straddle the foredeck with his kayak between himself and the rescuer (fig. 61). In this way the victim can assist with the repair by steadying his kayak and by holding onto the repair kit container.

The leader of the group should make sure that everybody's repair kit is accessible so the person doing the repairs can reach into someone else's kayak for a repair kit instead of having to retrieve his own from behind his seat.

If the hole is not too far underneath the hull, it is possible for the occupant of the damaged kayak to lean right over onto one side, supported by someone else, while a third person quickly dries the affected area and sticks a patch on.

60. Repairing a kayak at sea.

61. Assisting with a repair job. (Photo by the author.)

Towing

Towing can be hard, grueling work that nobody enjoys, but it is important to have the stamina to be able to tow someone should the need arise—and it usually arises in the worst possible conditions. It could be that one of your companions has been taken ill, is injured, or just overcome by fatigue. Whatever the reason, he is not going to make it back to shore under his own power, so he will have to be towed. To be able to tow him, you must have a towline, of course (see pp. 13–15).

Figure 62 shows five towing methods. The method you choose will depend on a number of factors, such as the distance involved, the strength of the rest of the group, the prevailing sea and weather conditions, the type of kayak you are paddling, and how straight the boat you are attempting to tow runs.

If a long haul is anticipated and the group is a strong one, two paddlers towing in tandem will have no difficulty in maintaining the speed of the main party (fig. 62A).

Leaders of small groups who are short of help must perform the tow with a single paddler (fig. 62B). A long towline is safer than a short one in rough water, especially in following seas.

For paddlers who are nervous and tired or those who might capsize at any moment, the safest way to tow them with limited assistance is to use a towline short enough to allow them to hold onto the stern of the towing kayak (fig. 62C). Paddling is difficult for the person towing, however, and the tandem method just described would be far less tiring.

With plenty of help, the easiest way of towing someone who needs constant support is to use two paddlers towing in tandem with a third paddler alongside supporting the person being towed (fig. 62D).

The method of getting an unconscious person to safety is illustrated in figure 62E. One paddler tows two kayaks across which the victim is laid. The kayakers in the rear hold on tightly to the victim, hold onto each other (to keep their kayaks together so a platform is maintained for the victim), and also hold their paddles in place with their elbows. Mouth-to-mouth resuscita-

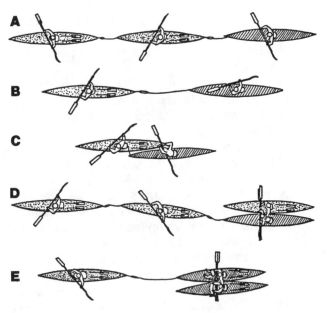

62. Methods for towing an ill or injured paddler.

tion could be carried out while on the move. Two people towing in tandem will make the tow more efficient.

Although most victims will eventually make it to shore, while they are being towed they immediately become an exposure risk. They may have been paddling for some time and therefore are wet with perspiration. The sudden inactivity and even a slight breeze will chill them down rapidly. Little can be done about this except to make certain the victim is adequately clothed.

Handling Dangerous Situations

Moored Vessels. Kayaks are ideal craft for exploring harbors, estuaries, and busy rivers—but beware of the dangers. One of the rules is keep away from the upstream end of moored vessels. Large ships are often berthed side by side and are separated only by buffers that leave a small gap of about one foot at the narrowest point. Anyone swept into this position is in great danger (see fig. 63).

To prevent himself from being swept into the narrowest position between the ships and either crushed by them or sucked underneath them and drowned, a victim must use his paddle, elbows, or arms to wedge

himself against the ships (fig. 63A). If the victim is alone, he stands little chance of surviving unless he can attract attention by shouting.

If the victim is accompanied by only one other kayaker, the other person must immediately go for help. This person may have to moor his boat and climb to the top of a quay to alert the ships involved so that a rope can be dropped down to the trapped paddler. (There are usually plenty of ladders leading up from the water level, though many of these are dilapidated and dangerous (fig. 63B).

If a group of kayakers is involved, a rescue can meanwhile be attempted by the leader or someone he designates. The rest of the group must hold position against the tidal flow well away from the danger area (fig. 63C). The rescuer should paddle toward the victim (fig. 63D) and throw a line in to him. If a line cannot be thrown to the victim, it can be attached to a life jacket or buoyancy aid and floated to him. If possible,

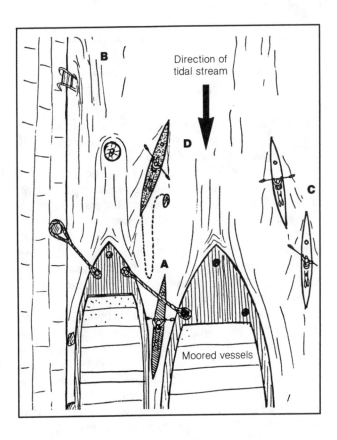

63. Rescue attempt of a kayaker trapped between two moored vessels.

64. Rope and flotation rescue attempt of a kayaker trapped against a fallen tree.

the victim should secure the line to his own deck line and allow it to run along the deck line toward the bow of his kayak as he is pulled out.

The rescuer's towline must have some means of quick release to be used should he also find himself in danger of being drawn between the vessels.

Fallen Trees. Although danger from fallen trees normally occurs on rapid rivers, similar difficulties can arise on tidal waters between closely packed islands. A kayaker who is careless or unaware of the dangers could find himself in the predicament depicted in figure 64. Not only is this a dangerous situation, it could be fatal. Just how bad things really are depends on the strength of the victim and the kind of grip he has on the tree, the force of the water pressing against him, how much of the tree is underneath the water, and the time it takes for help to arrive. The illustration shows rapidly moving water flowing against an old, fallen tree; however, the water does not have to be flowing fast, nor the tree dead. A highly respected kayak coach once referred to a weeping willow with green branches resting gently on the sur-

face of a slow-moving river as "whispering death"— how right he was!

Action must be taken quickly with these questions in mind:

- Can someone land on the bank without any great loss of valuable time?
- Is it possible for rescuers to climb along the tree?
- Is the victim in or out of his kayak?

If the victim is with a group of kayakers, the other kayakers can simultaneously attempt a rescue. One person can land, climb along the tree, and secure a holding rope around the victim. It may be necessary to fasten two ropes to the victim (see fig. 65), one to hold him in place and the other to be taken upstream from the tree so that his body can be pulled out and away from the tree that the water is forcing him against.

If the victim is still in the kayak, he may be held prisoner in the cockpit by water pressure, and it may be necessary to puncture the hull of the boat to release this pressure and the victim. If the rescuer is not carrying a strong diving knife or an ax, this can prove an almost impossible task.

In figure 65 the rescuer B has paddled into a position upstream where he is in no danger. The rescuer throws or floats a flotation device (for example, a life jacket) attached to a towline to the victim A. Unless the rescuer is very strong, it is almost impossible for him to tow the victim off the tree. It is better if a line is taken ashore and passed to someone who has a footing firm enough to insure that the pull is a positive one. It also might be possible to float a line down

65. When a kayaker is trapped against a fallen tree it may be necessary to secure the victim with one rope while pulling him away with another.

to the victim from the bank, but this will depend on the nature of the bank and how quickly a landing can be made.

Speed is vital. It takes only a minute or so for the victim to panic or tire and release his grip—assuming that he has been able to get a firm grip in the first place.

Any kayaker in danger of being trapped against a tree should throw his body over the trunk or nearest stout branch. He should twist his body so that the bottom of the hull of the kayak faces upstream. He should do everything possible to prevent the cockpit from turning to face upstream; if that should happen, he could become trapped and his life would be in imminent danger. Once the underside of the hull is facing upstream, he should release the spray cover and pull himself onto the tree. He must disregard the fate of the kayak until he is safely out of it.

To release a kayak that is trapped against a tree, the cockpit must be turned so that it faces downstream. In this way the water should drain out. It may be possible at this stage to lift the kayak out of the water. If not, a rope should be attached to the toggle nearest the bank and the boat should be pulled to shore.

Mud Flats and Quicksand. Kayakers must be especially careful when exploring very flat country in areas of heavy rainfall. These areas can be filled with bogs and quicksand. Likewise, when the tide drains from large flat estuaries and inlets, it can leave many miles of soft sand or leg-sucking mud. In some places the mud and sand may be deep and highly dangerous. Under no circumstances should a paddler leave his kayak. It will provide support in any conditions.

If faced with a large expanse of mud of unknown depth and consistency, a kayaker should either be patient and wait until the tide turns and floats him off, or drag the kayak behind him, testing the surface in front with the paddle.

A kayaker who does find himself waist deep in mud should first pull the kayak to him and use it for support. If it is obvious that the mud is too deep to walk across safely, he should sit astride the boat and slide it forward over the mud, making sure to stop moving it while there is still plenty of buoyant hull underneath. Next he must extricate his legs and hitch forward along the kayak before sliding the boat forward again. This can be slow, but a person in this situation will be quite safe so long as there is always some part of the kayak underneath him.

Remember at all times, keep calm, keep together, and keep the kayaks with you.

A person who is wandering the shore alone without his kayak and finds himself sinking into mud or sand should lie across the surface and attempt to move forward by "swimming" with a breaststroke.

Floating Ice.   Paddling near large lumps of ice or small icebergs is exciting and very pretty, but a person can become so engrossed that he is not aware of the dangers. Anyone who paddles close to a small iceberg may notice that at water level, the action of the warmer water near the surface undercuts it. The difference in temperature between the water and the ice also acts upon the submerged part of the iceberg. Gradually this will reduce it enough so that it may fracture underwater. This breaking off of ice is called calving.

As is well known, nine-tenths of an iceberg lies under the water. Calving throws this large volume of floating ice off-balance. It then takes up a completely different angle in the water or rolls over completely—spectacular to watch, but dangerous to be near.

If iceberg A in figure 66 calved at fracture point B, the kayakers could be killed by the new iceberg C. New icebergs have sharp, jagged profiles, which indicate that they have never rolled and should be treated with caution. Iceberg D is smooth and round. It has probably rolled at least once already and is much safer to approach.

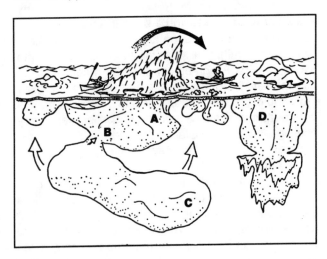

66. An iceberg ready to calve.

67. Kayakers following a shore lead look for a cutting in the ice shaft that will allow them to carry their boats ashore.

Whether an iceberg has calved recently is usually indicated by the amount it has been undercut. The deeper the undercut level with the surface, the longer it has been in the same position, and the more likely it will become unbalanced.

Kayakers should beware of extensive areas of floating ice. Although it may appear that there is plenty of paddle room between the pieces, any change of wind or tide could bring it all grinding and crushing together. If the ice is pack ice and therefore flat-topped, it might be possible to climb up onto the floating pieces. Progress can then be made by dragging the kayak along, jumping across the small gaps and paddling across the larger ones. When it comes time to launch again, a side drop may be necessary (see fig. 25, p. 30). Glacial ice, however, is almost impossible to climb on safely, due to its irregular shape and instability.

In some parts of the Arctic, ice along the shore can cause special problems. In figure 67 the paddlers are following a "shore lead," a gap between the floating ice and the shore. Although land is only a few yards away, an ice shelf that may run for many miles along a sandless, rocky shore makes it almost inaccessible.

The overhanging wall of hard blue ice is all that is left of sea pack ice, which, at some time, was attached to the shore. With an onshore wind, the kayakers in the illustration are at great risk, especially with a flooding tide. Landing is possible only where a small rivulet has cut through the ice toward the sea to form a cutting, up which kayaks and equipment can be carried to safety.

HANDLING DOUBLE KAYAKS

Double Kayaks

Because double kayaks can be sailed or slept in, long-distance journeys are not governed by the paddlers' waking hours. Meals can be taken or even cooked on the move. With lee boards down and mast up, it is possible to forget about paddling and sail a double quite successfully over quite long distances. Proof of all these points lies in the fact that the Atlantic Ocean has been crossed three times using double kayaks.

Because of its width, a double is sympathetic to slow responses and poor technique. Unfortunately, this means that after their introduction to the sport many doubles paddlers remain quite satisfied with a technical repertoire that consists of nothing more adventurous than a forward paddling stroke.

In certain areas and in sheltered conditions, doubles can be a good way of introducing some people to the delights of the open sea. If the instructor occupies the rearmost position, the student can be under observation at all times.

Double kayaks used on the open sea should exhibit certain qualities. Widths should be thirty to thirty-six inches and lengths nineteen to twenty-two feet. Short doubles of wide beam handle like slugs and should be avoided unless they are to be used as play boats. Deep-sea doubles should have enough volume to carry two people and all the equipment necessary for a prolonged trip in a wilderness area.

Cockpits or seating positions should separate clumsy and uncoordinated paddlers from their partners. This will prevent paddlers from clacking together and will preserve harmony.

When paddling, or in the event of a capsize, seats and thigh supports should be fixed firmly in position. For long-distance expedition work, however, it should be possible to remove them so that one or both occupants can wriggle down in their cockpits and shelter inside the hull.

From an economical point of view, a double kayak will cost less to buy than two single boats. But although it should paddle faster than a single, it will not paddle twice as fast, nor will it carry twice the equipment.

On your journeys you will never be short of company, but this can be a mixed blessing. Harmony comes with practice, and if it does not exist between the pair on land, it is not going to materialize on the water.

In rough conditions or in a capsize situation, it is worth remembering that all your eggs are in one basket. Because of this, all the deep-water rescues applicable to double kayaks should be practiced in controlled conditions and well in advance of a trip.

Fiberglass Double Kayaks. The Eddyline designed by Werner Furrer, the Sisiutle designed by Lee Moyer, and the Seascape designed by John Abbenhouse (fig. 68) are the only double kayaks I am familiar with that are available in either North America or the United Kingdom and that I would consider to be well-designed boats.

The Sisiutle can be purchased with three cockpits, but with this added facility paddling space is very limited. I think the center cockpit is best reserved for rescue purposes or for some small nonpaddling passenger. If the Sisiutle is to be used on rough water, I would suggest that the seats be secured more firmly to the hull of the boat. For those who like steeply angled decks, those on the Sisiutle have excellent water-shedding properties.

The Eddyline is an extremely comfortable kayak to paddle and is a very seaworthy craft. I have also seen it carry a sail to good advantage. I consider its molded bucket seats much more practical than the loose-fitting variety.

The Seascape is a newcomer to the doubles scene and is a welcome addition. It has a powerful, seaworthy bow that rises well to choppy seas, and the large volume hull makes it possible for the occupants to be self-sufficient for long periods. In its appearance and seaworthiness, the Seascape resembles the ancient two-manhole baidarkas more than any other double kayak that I have seen on the market.

Folding Double Kayaks. There are a number of folding kayaks on the market, and the two most popular designs are made in Europe. The Klepper, made in Germany, is an old favorite. It is carried in two bags, and when assembled it makes a double kayak seventeen feet long by thirty-five inches wide. The one-man version is fifteen feet long by twenty-eight inches wide. The frames are of mountain ash

joined by fittings of aluminum. The whole affair is covered with a skin of Hypalon and canvas. Air-filled sponsons are incorporated into the cover, which will float the kayak in the event of a capsize. The Klepper has a considerable freeboard, and this could prove difficult in high winds.

The Nautiraid, made in France, is a beautifully built kayak with a slightly lower freeboard than the Klepper. It, too, has sponsons as part of its integral design, but these do not influence the tension of the cover as they do in the Klepper. The double version contains fourteen pieces, which can be put together in just over a quarter of an hour. The completed double is sixteen feet, six inches long by thirty-six inches wide, but the kayak is designed so that it can be used by a single paddler. The Nautiraid single is short by seagoing standards—only thirteen feet, six inches long by thirty inches wide. However, like the Klepper, it comes equipped with a rudder that compensates for any tendency to yaw.

The most revolutionary folding design I have ever seen is the Feathercraft, which comes from Canada. It is the brainchild of Doug Simpson of Vancouver, who has abandoned traditional materials like wood and canvas in favor of more modern substances. The result is a folding kayak that is lighter, quicker, easier to assemble, and easier to care for. The frame consists of high-tensile aluminum tubing. The longitudinal members are shock corded like tent poles for easy assembly. These attach to a welded cockpit. Once the frame is together and the cover is in place, the stern deck bar is hinged and becomes the tool used to expand the frame lengthwise, thus tensioning the skin. The hull material consists of a layer of Butyl rubber sandwiched between two layers of woven nylon. The deck is made of waterproofed nylon pack cloth, and the spray cover is sewn directly onto the deck to become a part of it. Like other folding kayaks the Feathercraft has air sponsons built into the gunwales.

The Feathercraft comes in a single as well as a double version. The single is a sensible fourteen feet, eight inches long and twenty-six inches wide and weighs a mere thirty-eight pounds. The double is eighteen feet long by thirty-two inches wide and weighs fifty pounds. The Feathercraft is portable. The frame breaks down to form a backpack that includes shoulder straps and a hip belt.

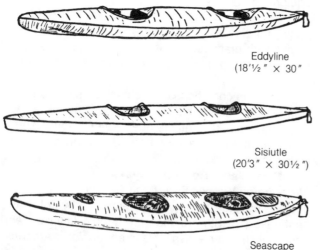

Eddyline
(18′½″ × 30″)

Sisiutle
(20′3″ × 30½″)

Seascape
(20′ × 3″)

68. The Eddyline and Sisiutle double kayaks.

Paddles

Doubles have wider, fuller hulls than single boats, and because of this I prefer to use a paddle at least a foot longer than the one I would normally use in a single. Some paddlers like them even longer, and this is especially preferable if a rudder is not being used.

Packing

Because a double is by necessity a roomy craft, it can beget or encourage disorganized packing. I am a great believer in dividing a kayak into watertight compartments with watertight access hatches and some kind of bailing pump as part of the everyday equipment. This gives the occupants the responsibility of considering the order and method of storage.

Safety

Naturally, all safety considerations that apply to single craft apply to the double. Boats should be equipped with taut deck lines, paddle parks, chart and compass, elastics and towlines, flares, and first aid and repair kits for both day trips and long-distance journeys.

Technique

The techniques required of the double kayaker are basically the same as those of the paddler of single craft. However, the two paddlers often perform different strokes at the same time and, done properly, in synchronization.

Ideally paddling should be done in unison, but with inexperienced partners this can be more a dream than a reality. It is important that each paddler understands the role of the other. Close to shore or when dodging rocks, the person at the front is the pilot, and it is he who keeps the "captain" or stern paddler informed as to what is going on up ahead. It is the job of the stern paddler to steer and direct the boat, while the bow paddler keeps the kayak moving through the water at a steady speed by maintaining his forward stroke. So that teamwork can develop between partners, pairs should paddle together over varying distances, and under diverse sea conditions.

Although any change of direction should be done by the stern paddler in doubles kayaking, track deviation is probably best corrected by using a rudder. This eliminates the necessity of leaning the boat over onto one side—a more difficult maneuver with two paddlers than with one.

Launching

A double kayak can be launched in the same manner as a single kayak. Less strain will be placed on the hull, however, if the bow paddler is settled into position first while the fore-end of the boat is supported by the water.

If the beach slopes steeply and the water is calm, the kayak can be placed parallel to the shore and the paddles used for support while you enter the boat.

Forward Paddling

Once partners acquire a little harmony and develop an easy, relaxed forward paddle stroke, daily cruising distance should be equal to, if not better than a single kayak's ten to fifteen miles on an easy day or twenty to twenty-five miles with a little effort.

Turning and Maneuvering

The stern paddler can make small changes in direction or corrections of track by applying ruddering strokes when necessary. If more help is needed, the bow paddler can assist by paddling slightly harder on the opposite side from which you wish to turn. In this manner, corrections are done without any loss of forward speed.

Turning Through 360 Degrees. Turning through 360 degrees requires the sweep and reverse sweep strokes, which are performed by both paddlers in unison. The bow paddler sweeps out on the side opposite to which the turn is to be made. At the same time, the stern paddler executes a reverse sweep on the side opposite to the bow paddler's stroke (fig. 69A). If the strokes are done with equal force and

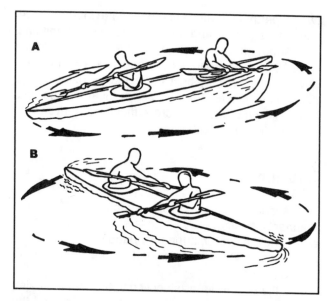

69. The reverse and sweep strokes, performed simultaneously on opposite sides, will turn a double kayak through 360 degrees.

simultaneously, the kayak will pivot around easily in a graceful turn (fig. 69B). A normal draw stroke, performed simultaneously on opposite sides by both paddlers, will turn a stationary double.

Fast Turn. As the name implies, the fast turn or low telemark (fig. 70) can be done successfully only when the kayak is moving forward fast—the faster the better. On a prearranged signal, the paddlers stop their forward stroke and place their paddle blades out into the water with their leading edge high. The paddles will plane on the surface of the water and will be in a position to support both the paddlers, who now lean over into the turn putting the gunwale underwater. The kayak will turn quickly and in a spectacular manner. As the forward speed decreases, however, both paddlers must sweep their

70. The fast turn or low telemark.

paddles forward, so that they finish sitting in an upright position.

Reverse Sweep and Bow Rudder. As the kayak moves forward, the stern paddler performs a reverse sweep on one side while the bow paddler executes what is called a bow rudder—the paddle is placed well out from the side with the driving face of the blade facing in toward the bow. The bow paddler's

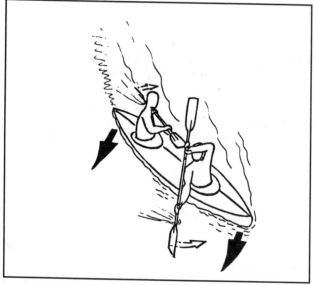

71. To move diagonally sideways, the stern paddler performs a reverse sweep on one side, while the bow paddler performs a bow rudder on the opposite side.

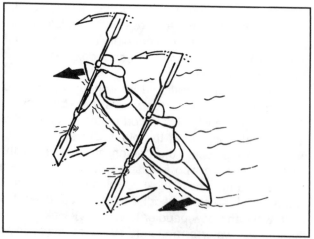

72. The draw stroke.

thumbs point upward (fig. 71). The reverse sweep and bow rudder complement each other, and the kayak moves diagonally sideways in the direction of the paddle. If the bow paddler inadvertently draws the driving face of his paddle inward, instead of holding it steady, the stroke then becomes a bow draw. This is not really what you want to do because the bow draw is a very strong stroke, strong enough to halt the diagonal movement of the kayak and turn the kayak's bow in the direction of the paddle. Practice on the part of the bow paddler will result in a good, nonretarding bow rubber.

Draw Stroke. Doubles can be moved sideways in exactly the same way as a single kayak, using the draw stroke (fig. 72). As with all other double strokes, it is important that both paddlers stroke together. Otherwise the kayak will turn instead of moving sideways.

A good draw stroke may be necessary when positioning for a rescue or when caving, dodging rocks, or just coming alongside.

Deep-Water Rescues

Anyone can capsize. You may feel stable and secure in your nice, wide double kayak when most of your paddling is done on fairly flat water, and because of this a capsize will be all the more disturbing when it comes. I would advise pairs who paddle together regularly to practice their emergency drills in calm, warm water before paddling off into the open sea. Make sure you keep your paddles under control. If you have done your packing correctly, you should not see any of your equipment floating out of the cockpit. For added stability, the paddle float can be used with any of the rescues and reentries described below.

Rescue of an Unescorted Double Kayak. First the kayak must be turned the right way up, with as little water as possible allowed to collect inside. To do this the two paddlers should position themselves on the same downwind side of the boat and near the center. At a signal, they both lift and flip the kayak over and away from themselves, thus scooping up as little water as possible into the cockpit.

The stern paddler should enter first so that he can watch and steady the kayak while reentry is made into the forward cockpit. There are two ways of doing this. As one paddler holds the bow tightly, the other pulls himself up onto the reardeck and hitches along

toward the nearest cockpit (fig. 73). This method can be tricky in rough conditions. A second and more positive method is for the bow paddler to steady the kayak by hanging on to one side of the stern cockpit while the stern paddler climbs in from the other side (fig. 74A). The stern paddler then sculls for support while his partner reenters (fig. 74B).

Once both paddlers are back in position, it is worth remembering that they are now facing the conditions that capsized them in the first place. Because of this, one paddler must maintain the support stokes while the other gets to work and attempts to bail the boat dry.

73. One method of reentering the kayak after a capsize.

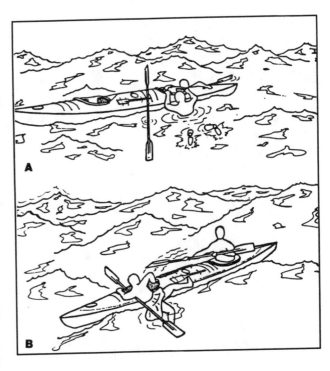

74. An effective method of reentry is for the stern paddler to enter first (A) and then scull for support while the bow paddler reenters (B).

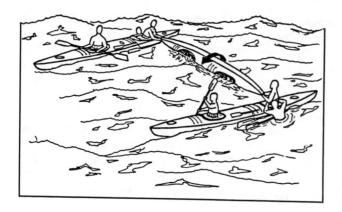

75. The H rescue is a method of emptying a double kayak.

It is possible for each paddler to have his own bailer and to pump the kayak out together. The paddles are supported across the shoulders, and the occupants scull together on opposite sides. In this way the boat will be emptied in half the time.

H Deep-Water Rescue of an Escorted Kayak. For some years now, the H rescue has not been used by paddlers of single kayaks as a method of emptying an upturned boat. This is because the occupants of the rescuing boats, who had to heave up and down on a kayak half-full of water, had difficultly staying upright. Holding the boats parallel was an additional problem. With doubles, these problems do not exist, and the H rescue (fig. 75) is an ideal way of emptying any escorted double that is not intolerably weighted down with expedition equipment. Any tendency on the part of the rescue craft to swing around can be corrected by the paddler not involved in the lifting. If the water is very cold, the paddlers can sit on the decks of the rescuing craft and assist by sculling for support on one side. The methods of reentry are similar to those used for solo craft. The easiest method is for a double to pull alongside an already righted craft so the two seated paddlers can hold onto the empty cockpits and steady the boat for the two swimming paddlers to reenter, one at a time.

NAVIGATION

Navigation is a highly specialized subject, and the more ambitious your sea kayaking, the more you should know. The following aspects are particularly useful to the kayaker.

Nautical charts are the basic tool for planning any kind of adventurous sea trip. They are the maps of the sea, and with only a little practice they will soon become a joy to look at and to use.

Scales

The relation between the distance on a chart and the distance over the surface of the earth is called the scale. The larger the scale of the chart, the smaller the area of the globe it will cover.

Chart scales can vary, but for coastal paddling a suitable scale would be between 1:50,000 and 1:150,000. If you fancy doing some harbor exploration, a scale of 1:10,000 would give you more local detail—the larger the scale on the chart, the more detail will be shown.

Normally charts are very accurate, but if you decide to explore some of the more remote areas of the world you might find that the details given on the map bear little or no relationship to what is shown on the chart. Until I paddled along the Bering Sea coast of the Aleutian Islands, I thought that all nautical charts were scribed by the hand of God. It was only when I discovered that a river that was supposed to run into Blackstone Bay on Umnak Island did not exist that I realized that this was not the case.

A chart can be a little confusing at first glance because of all the tiny figures on that part of the chart that represents the sea. These are the depth soundings. On older charts, the soundings are given in fathoms and feet (one fathom equals six feet). Most charts are now metric, however, and have their soundings in meters and decimeters, e.g., 103 for 10.3 meters. All soundings on charts are taken from a point below which the tide is unlikely to fall, called the chart datum. This is the level of the lowest astronomical tide. On your chart you will find that dry land is shaded a buff color, but any area awash at high tide and dry at low tide is colored a nice seaweed green. These drying heights are also marked in meters and decimeters underlined and show the height above chart datum to which the area dries. It would be worth your while to obtain the booklet of chart symbols and abbreviations, sold where you purchase nautical charts.

Some information marked on the charts is of direct interest to the ocean paddler. This includes any changes in depths, drying heights, and the quality of the sea bottom (possibly indicating a long walk in deep mud at low tide), tide races and overfalls, whirlpools, speed and direction of the tidal stream, types of shoreline, positions of buoys marking the navigation channels for large shipping, and conspicuous buildings and so on that can be used as transit markers.

To measure distance across the chart, use the scale at the side—one minute of latitude equals one sea mile. A long piece of fine, thin chain is good for laying on the chart to obtain distances because its flexibility will enable it to go in and out of small bays and around headlands. Use only a soft lead pencil so that any marks can be removed without spoiling the surface of the chart.

I find two set squares easier to use than a parallel rule. If you intend to use dividers, obtain a good pair with fine points—fingernail scratching on the edge of a torn-off cigarette packet is not really setting a good example in equipment preparedness.

Charts should be kept dry and in good condition. If you intend to carry yours on the foredeck directly in front of you, seal it inside a special transparent waterproof chart bag made for the purpose, or cut the chart into convenient-sized portions and cover each piece on both sides with a self-adhesive, transparent, waterproof covering.

If you intend to paddle in a wilderness area, I would recommend that you study the relevant topographical maps and include them in your equipment.

Bearings. On your chart you will see what is called a compass rose. The geographic or true north is parallel to the lines of longitude, which run from the top to the bottom of the chart. The compass you use on the deck of your kayak, however, will point to what is called magnetic north. The difference between this magnetic north and true north is known as the magnetic variation. This variation is not constant and it varies depending upon its position on the earth's surface or the passing of time. To discover the variation for the area in which you intend to paddle you need only consult the appropriate chart. This variation will be printed on the compass roses that are placed strategically across the chart. You will see that it is expressed in degrees either east or west of the true north meridian. If you find that you have to convert a "true bearing" to a magnetic one or vice versa, follow these guidelines: magnetic to true—add the easterly variation; true to magnetic—subtract the easterly variation.

Remember that when you are heaping equipment upon your foredeck, your compass can be influenced by any close object that gives off a magnetic disturbance. Diving knives and transistor radios should therefore be kept away.

Tides

To the casual onlooker sitting on the beach, the water moved by the tide appears to travel only up and down the sand. Linked, however, with this rise and fall are the horizontal movements of the water. These are known as the tidal streams. Far out to sea these streams have little effect, but close inshore where most paddling takes place, their effect can be quite pronounced. By studying the tidal streams, however, and using them carefully, the ocean paddler can make these water movements do a good deal of the work for him. A tidal stream flowing parallel to a coastline can make a journey half as tiring. If the stream runs past a headland its speed will increase. It will slow down again as it runs along a bay. If the bay is well indented, be careful when you paddle close inshore lest you find yourself sweating against a back eddy that is running in the opposite direction along the shoreline. When paddling against the tide, these back eddies can prove very useful.

If, as you paddle along, you come across a place where a fast tidal stream crosses over an underwater shelf or ridge, you will see waves breaking steeply like those on a rapid river. This is called an overfall, and unless you are proficient at paddling in surf, this type of disturbance will prove very dangerous. If by some unfortunate mischance the wind happens to be blowing against the tide, you may find the conditions almost suicidal.

The tidal streams that flow around some coastlines are complicated, but they flow in predictable patterns. Because these patterns are predictable, their direction and strength at different times can be published. Tide tables can be obtained from boat chandlers, and there are basically two sources where the speed of a tidal stream can be obtained: from a chart—small-feathered arrows show the flood stream and unfeathered arrows depict the ebb stream; from a *Tidal Stream Atlas.*

The trouble with the information given in the *Tidal Stream Atlas* is that it gives only the speeds for areas several miles offshore. Charts, on the other hand, tend to show more localized tidal speeds, but a certain amount of experience is needed to work out exactly what will happen close inshore. There tidal movement is influenced by headlands, which will increase the speed somewhat, and the presence of islands, which tend to constrict the tidal flow and increase the speed even further.

Tidal predictions are not accurate because the times of high and low water can be influenced by such variables as barometric pressure, high winds,

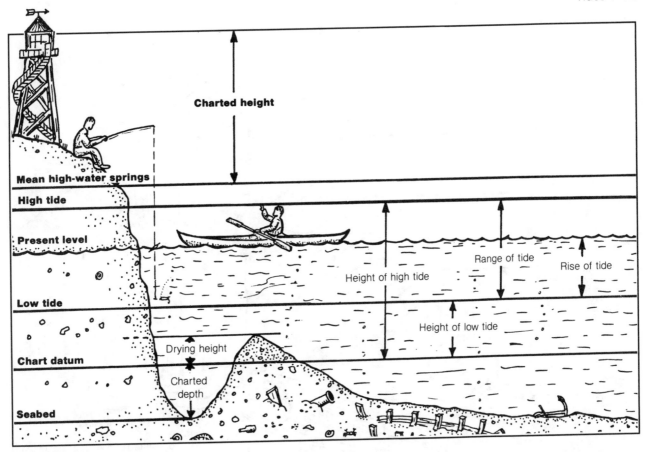

Charted height

Mean high-water springs

High tide

Present level

Range of tide

Rise of tide

Height of high tide

Low tide

Height of low tide

Drying height

Chart datum

Charted depth

Seabed

76. Tidal range.

and (in an estuary) heavy rains and melting snows. Storm surges (caused by the passage of a sudden depression) such as those that occur in the southern North Sea can oscillate the level of the sea. Coupled with gale force winds and a tide that is abnormally high, storm surges can cause widespread flooding.

Tides (see fig. 76) are caused by the gravitational pull of the moon and, to a lesser extent, the sun. The moon and sun together exert their greatest pull when they are in conjunction (sun directly behind the moon—new moon), or in opposition (on opposite sides of the earth—full moon). The tidal range is greater at this period, and these are known as spring tides. When the moon and sun are at right angles to each other (in quadrature) there is a lesser influence, and consequently a lesser tidal range, known as neap tides. Spring and neap tides occur every week alternately throughout the year.

On 22 March and 22 or 23 September annually the sun crosses the equator, and its declination is zero. The spring tides occurring at this time are greater than normal, and you should take care if you intend to plan trips at this period, known as "the equinox" because day and night are equal.

Because tidal streams are faster flowing during spring tides, your passage will be easier and quicker with the tide or more difficult paddling against it. Any adverse conditions—for instance a wind blowing against the tide, or the stream rushing over shallows—will be worsened by spring tides.

On the open sea, a change in the direction of the tidal stream does not always coincide with the time of high water (HW) and low water (LW), and you may find the tide running in the flood direction perhaps as much as two hours after the ebb has started, or vice versa. The difference between HW and LW each day along the coast is six hours thirteen minutes. The time of HW is approximately fifty minutes later each day.

When the direction of the tidal stream changes, it is said to be "slack water," although this may not

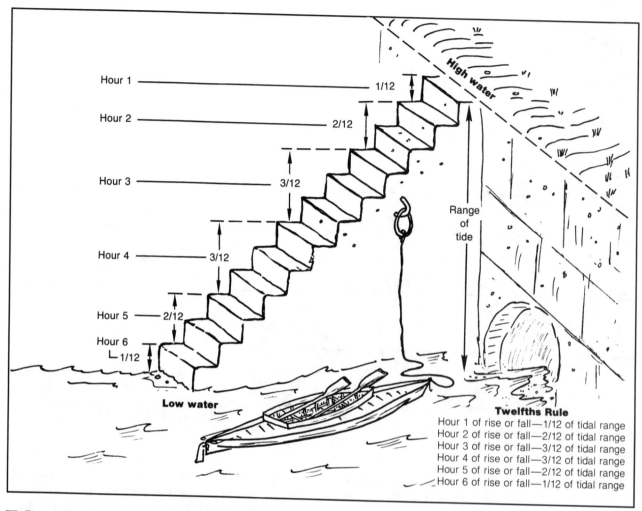

Hour 1 ——————— 1/12

Hour 2 ——————— 2/12

Hour 3 ——————— 3/12

Hour 4 ——————— 3/12

Hour 5 — 2/12

Hour 6
└ 1/12

High water

Range
of
tide

Low water

Twelfths Rule
Hour 1 of rise or fall—1/12 of tidal range
Hour 2 of rise or fall—2/12 of tidal range
Hour 3 of rise or fall—3/12 of tidal range
Hour 4 of rise or fall—3/12 of tidal range
Hour 5 of rise or fall—2/12 of tidal range
Hour 6 of rise or fall—1/12 of tidal range

77. The twelfths rule helps the paddler understand the variation in the rate of rise and fall of tides.

last for very long. The twelfths rule (see fig. 77) tells us that the level of water does not rise or fall at a constant rate throughout the six-hour period between LW and HW and between HW and LW. The greatest rate of rise or fall (and hence the strongest tidal stream) occurs halfway through the tide in open water. In rivers and estuaries, the greatest rate occurs soon after the stream has commenced to run in the new direction.

Currents

There are also water movements within the sea, but their origins are thermal rather than lunar. Conse-

quently their direction never changes. Currents have a much smaller influence on the sea paddler than do tidal streams.

Transits

The time-honored method of navigation by transits has two great advantages: it is simple and exact. For these reasons and because of the presence of objects, the system is of more practical use to the coastal paddler than any other. The principle is simply that of keeping two objects in line, one behind the other, and observing their movement in relation to each other. In figure 78 paddler A has the buoy in line

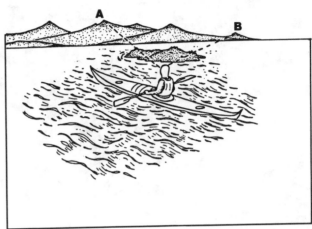

78. Transits help the paddler to determine whether he is making headway against winds or tides.

79. Any object can be used as a transit marker.

with the lighthouse. Because the buoy and the lighthouse stay relatively in line with each other, he knows that he is drifting neither one way nor the other. If however, the objects appear to move apart from each other, he knows he is traveling or drifting in the direction that the marker farthest away is opening up in relation to the nearer marker. Paddler B has observed that the lighthouse appears to have moved to the right in relation to the buoy; because of this he knows that he is drifting to the right.

It is particularly important to understand transits in order to determine whether you are making headway against an adverse wind or tide. The paddler in figure 79 has a hummock of grass lined up with the hill A in the background. He is also using a nearby hummock of grass lined up with the hill B on the far headland. By watching these objects move in relation to one another, he can take heart that he is not standing still against the adverse conditions.

Any object can be used as a transit marker, and it is part of the art to change marks constantly as the need arises.

If you have to pinpoint your position over, say, a wreck or a reef, the intersection of straight lines drawn through two sets of transit markers will do the job exactly. As an ocean paddler, you should work at becoming transit-conscious as soon as possible by relating the transit marks on your chart with the objects around you on the sea and on the land.

Buoyage

Anyone who paddles out onto estuaries or the open sea should become familiar with the various systems of buoyage that are designed to keep regular ocean traffic moving safely and smoothly in restricted waters. They can also help keep the seas free from upturned, empty kayaks. Knowledge of buoyage will help the ocean paddler locate his position accurately in bad conditions and will enable him to make decisions that take into account local shipping movements.

If you must enter busy shipping lanes, keep the intrusion to a minimum and cherish the thought that some ships take up to ten miles to stop. Unless someone were looking over the side they would not even know they hit you.

Ships turning around buoys at high speed will skid a considerable distance sideways. A wall of steel and rivets approaching at, say, six to ten knots can make even the bravest paddler feel uneasy. Make yourself familiar with the idiosyncrasies of local shipping movements so that you are not caught out.

In 1982 most of the maritime nations of the world

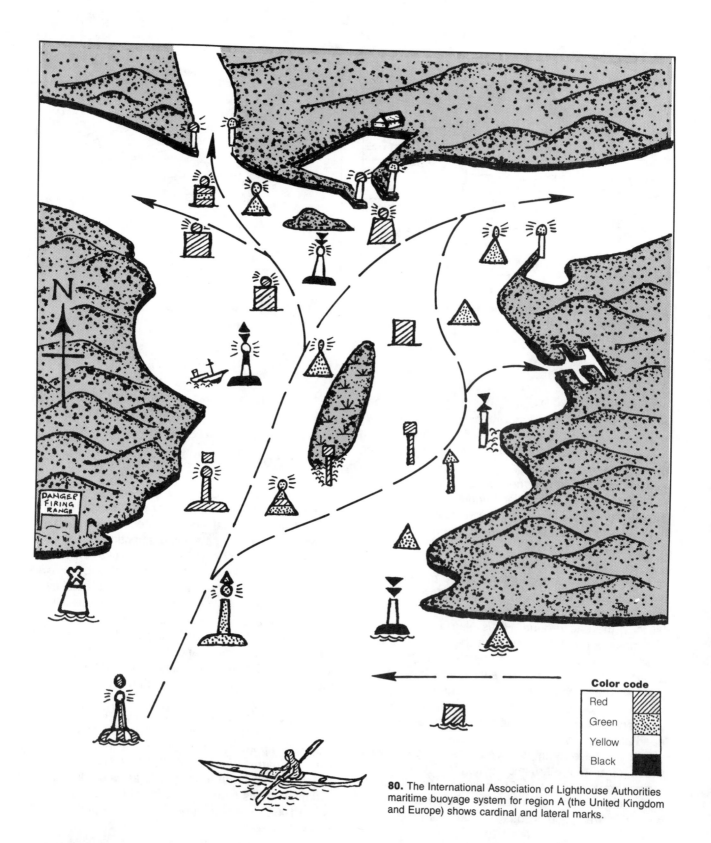

80. The International Association of Lighthouse Authorities maritime buoyage system for region A (the United Kingdom and Europe) shows cardinal and lateral marks.

Color code

Red	
Green	
Yellow	
Black	

DANGER
FIRING
RANGE

N

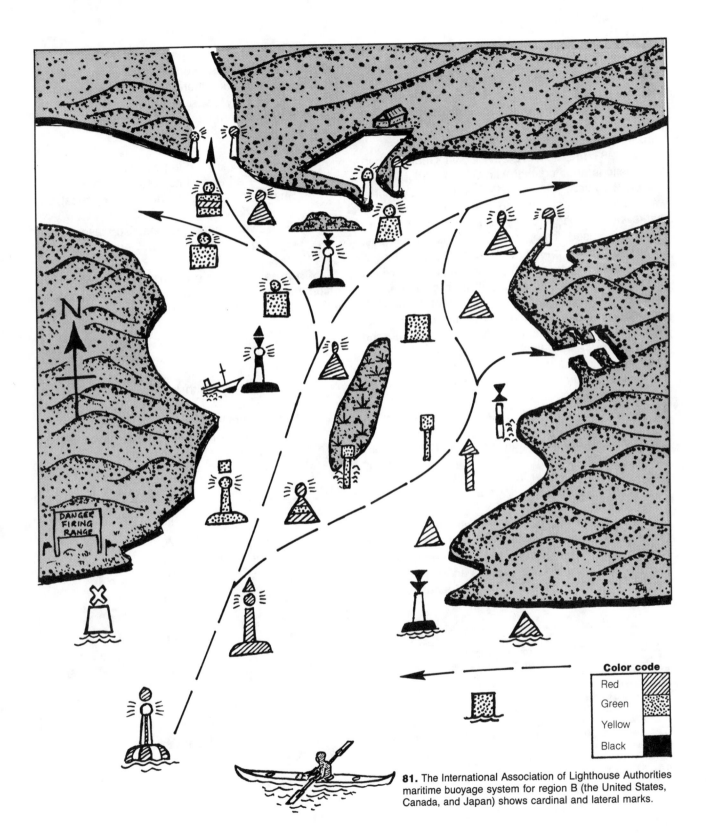

81. The International Association of Lighthouse Authorities maritime buoyage system for region B (the United States, Canada, and Japan) shows cardinal and lateral marks.

Color code

Red
Green
Yellow
Black

N

DANGER
FIRING
RANGE

signed an agreement sponsored by the International Association of Lighthouse Authorities with a view to standardizing aids to navigation. The United Kingdom and Europe subscribe to the Region A system (see fig. 80): port-hand day marks are red, starboard are green. All colors apply when approaching from seaward. (See the color code in fig. 80 inset.)

In 1983 the United States Coast Guard began modifications and, together with Canada, adopted the Region B system (see fig. 81). Port-hand day marks were changed from black to green—starboard-hand marks were already red—and white lights were no longer to be used on port or starboard navigation aids.

Isolated Danger Marks. An isolated danger mark is a pillar or buoy over an isolated danger which has navigable water all around it. If an awareness of your position and of dangers is important during daylight hours, it is vital during the hours of darkness. Because of this, you should acquaint yourself with the most common light-flashing sequences and their chart abbreviations (fig. 82).

Isolated danger marks are coded as follows:

Topmark—Two black spheres, one above the other.
Color—Black with one or more broad horizontal bands.
Shape—Pillar or spar.
Light—White, Gp. fl. (two).

Safe Water Marks. Safe water marks indicate that there is navigable water all around the mark; these include center line marks and midchannel marks. Such a mark may also be used as an alternative to a cardinal or a lateral mark to indicate a landfall.

Special marks are yellow, but they are not normally of interest to the paddler unless used as a traffic separation mark where use of a conventional channel mark may cause confusion. Sometimes a yellow buoy marks the seaward extremity of an army firing range.

Topmark (if any)—Single red sphere.
Color—Red and white vertical stripes.
Shape—Spherical, pillar with spherical topmark or spar.
Light (when fitted)—White, isophase, occulting or one long flash every ten seconds.

Channel Separation Marks. Channel separation marks are positioned where a channel divides. If the preferred channel is to port the description is as follows:

Topmark—Single green cone, pointed upwards.
Color—Green with a broad horizontal red band.
Shape (buoy)—Cone, pillar, or spar.
Light—Color green. Composite group flashing (two plus one).

▭▭▭▭▭ (F.) Fixed continuous light
▬ ▬ ▬ ▬ (Fl.) Flashing regular intervals
▪▪▪ ▪▪▪ (Gp. Fl.) Flashing in groups
▮▮▮▮▮▮▮▮▮▮ (V. Qk. Fl.) Very quick flash (100 or 120 per minute)
▪ ▪ ▪ ▪ ▪ ▪ (Qk. Fl.) Quick flash (50 or 60 per minute)
▬▬ ▬ ▬ ▬ (Occ.) Occulting light longer than dark
▬▬▬ ▬▬▬ (Gp. Occ.) Group occulting
▭▭ ▭▭ ▭▭ (Iso.) Isophase equal periods of light and dark
(Alt.) Alternating steady light, changing color
(Dir.) Directional light, a steady light
(Long fl.) Light not less than two-second durations

82. Common light-flashing sequences.

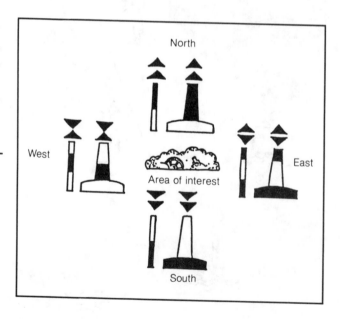

83. Cardinal marks.

If the preferred channel is to starboard the description is as follows:

Topmark—Single red cylinder or can.
Color—Red with a broad horizontal green band.
Shape (buoy)—Cylindrical (can) pillar or spar.
Light—Color red. Composite group flashing (two plus one).

Cardinal Marks. Cardinal marks (see fig. 83) are laid to indicate that the deepest water is on the named side of the mark, or which is the safe side to pass danger; e.g., a north cardinal mark is passed to the north (i.e., you must leave the mark to the south of you). A kayaker may well do the opposite, and so avoid being in an area that larger vessels are navigating.

North cardinal mark:
Topmark—Two black cones, one above the other, points upwards.
Color—Black above yellow.
Shape—Pillar or spar.
Light (when fitted)—White, V. Qk. Fl.(b) or Qk. Fl. (c).

East cardinal mark:
Topmark—Two black cones, one above the other, base-to-base.
Color—Black with a single broad horizontal yellow band.
Shape—Pillar or spar.
Light (when fitted)—White, V. Qk. Fl. (three) every five seconds or Qk. Fl. (three) every ten seconds.

South cardinal mark:
Topmark—Two black cones, one above the other, points downward.
Color—Yellow above black.
Shape—Pillar or spar.
Light (when fitted)—White, V. Qk. Fl. (six) plus long flash(d) every ten seconds or Qk. Fl. (six) plus long flash(d) every fifteen seconds.

West cardinal mark:
Topmark—Two black cones, one above the other, point to point.
Color—Yellow with a single broad horizontal black band.
Shape—Pillar or spar.

Light (when fitted)—White, V. Qk. Fl. (nine) every ten seconds or Qk. Fl. (nine) every fifteen seconds.

Coastal Problems

Reading Charts. With a little practice, a quick look at a chart should give you an overall picture of an area. Charts are designed for those who go to sea in much larger craft, and the ocean paddler must therefore cultivate an ability to read between the lines. Figure 84 shows what could be a typical and interesting piece of coastline for exploration.

An experienced kayaker looking at the chart on which figure 84 is based might make the following observations.

In a heavy swell, only the north end of the bay will give any hope of a trouble-free landing (fig. 84A). The approaches to the bay may be made more difficult by a race off the headland. If the bottom is shelving there will be an associated overfall. The small sheltered inlet on the south side of the island (fig. 84B) would make a good landing place, but if the island is a small one beware of the swell that sweeps around and causes rough water by colliding in the approaches to your landing place.

In an emergency only, the north end of the unprotected beach might be used by a proficient group (fig. 84C). The bay (fig. 84D) is dangerous—because of its size, the beach probably slopes steeply, causing dumping surf. In any sort of a swell, this bay could be used only in an extreme emergency and with great care. A harbor (fig. 84E) provides the classic protection for shipping, but very small craft should take time to study the approaches as best they can from the seaward. The north pier receives the main force of the swell, which collides with the wall. The waves are then reflected directly back into the swells, which come up behind. The size of the swell will govern the size of dangerous clapotis (waves caused by the colliding walls of water). These areas are very hazardous, and you should steer well clear of them.

Take care when entering between piers (fig. 84F); there may be an extensive area of turbulent water known as the "bar" where the river water meets the open sea (and probably a fast tidal stream). If you have taken time to plan your trip, you should enter the harbor on a flooding tide. If you have mistimed your

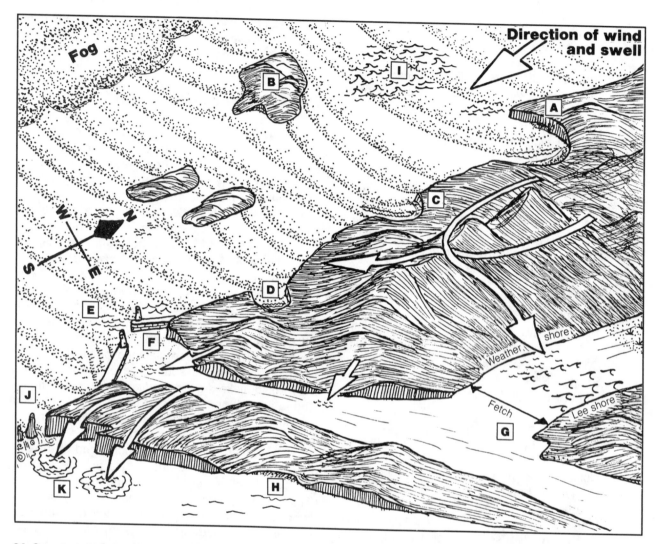

84. Some typical coastal problems, which the experienced paddler would foresee by studying a chart.

entrance, however, you may have a battle against an ebb stream on your hands. When leaving harbor, the south side of the pier would be best given a wide berth. Although not so violent as the direct clapotis, the angle of these reflected waves will cause the waves to peak up steeply and high, making your kayak pirouette on the crests, with perhaps most of your kayak hanging in fresh air—a good place to practice white-water technique.

Fetch is the distance across open water over which the wind blows without hindrance (fig. 84G). The height of the waves caused by the wind is governed by the wind's speed and the fetch. If you are paddling a little way offshore, the fetch may be only a few hundred feet if the wind is coming from the direction of the shore, and even though it may be gale force the waves will be comparatively small. This is known as a weather shore. If the wind is blowing onto shore, this is known as a lee shore. The fetch could be many hundreds of miles, creating big surf and dangerous landing conditions.

The beach (fig. 84H) is an ideal landing place on a weather shore with a gently shelving beach and easy access inland.

In blustery weather, all shoals and shallows (fig. 84I) must be viewed with caution. If the swells are large, shoals will be marked by breaking seas. Tidal streams also move faster over these shallow areas, and when these streams drain out between sandbanks they have a tendency to flow at right angles to the general direction you may have seen predicted in the *Tidal Stream Atlas.*

Take care when negotiating small isolated groups of rocks or pillars (fig. 84J) off exposed headlands, especially in heavy swells. They receive the full force of the tidal streams, which will increase in speed as the water flow is constricted. If the normal tidal streams are exceptionally fast, large, dangerous swirls and eddies can be caused after the stream has passed through.

Even when you have left the worst of the weather behind and think you are now paddling on sheltered waters, be especially careful at the base of mountains and high cliffs (fig. 84K). Localized gusts can hit downward with great violence, causing multiple capsizes among unsuspecting beginners.

Wind. Things are not always what they seem to be, and even the general direction of the wind can be deflected and contorted by the topography of the land. Nor should the general direction of the wind be confused with localized sea breezes, which will have far more effect on your paddling pleasure. The effect of these sea breezes is not usually felt more than ten miles or so offshore. The cause is simple. The land is

The Beaufort Wind Scale

Beaufort Number	Speed (Knots)	General Description	Energy or Wind Pressure	Sea	Kayaker's Criterion
0		Calm.	0	Sea like mirror.	Suitable for initial training from "safe" beaches.
1	1–3	Light air.	4	Ripples appear.	
2	4–6	Light breeze.	18	Tiny waves. No breaking crests.	
3	7–10	Gentle breeze.	50	Small waves. Crests begin to form.	Life gets interesting for all. Good for practicing capsize drill. Getting tough for beginners.
4	11–16	Moderate breeze.	128	Medium waves building up. Some white horses.	About the limit for the proficiency test standard paddlers on journey.
5	17–21	Fresh breeze.	220	Decidedly lumpy sea. Many white horses.	Anybody over proficiency standard enjoys this. Usually creates very good surf.
6	22–27	Strong breeze.	364	Large waves everywhere. Continually white horses.	Short journeys by advanced kayakers all right, but you are reaching the borderline.
7	28–33	Near gale.	544	Sea piles up. Spindrift off tops of waves.	Surf tends to be big. Experts are beginning to swear.
8	34–40	Gale.	800	The difference from a landsman's view of these is difficult to say except that the sea looks lumpy, high breaking waves and spindrift following the wind path.	Surf gets to be very big, and you spend your time hanging on to your tent.
9	41–47	Strong gale.	1104		
10	48–55	Storm.	1512		Surf enormous, and you get blown away with your tent.

Formula for kinetic energy: $E = \frac{1}{2}MV^2$ when E = Energy
M = Mass
V = Velocity

85. The Beaufort Wind Scale.

heated by the sun until its temperature is higher than that of the sea. The heated air over the land rises rapidly, causing the cool air over the sea to rush in and take its place (often with its accompanying fog.)

These onshore breezes can be quite strong—a strong breeze on the Beaufort Wind Scale (fig. 85) has a mean wind speed of approximately twenty-five knots. Because many of these localized winds are predictable, the cautious paddler can time his trips accordingly by either utilizing the relative stillness of the mornings or evenings or by timing more long-distance expeditions on a seasonal basis and waiting for the spring or fall. In some areas, winter brings most settled weather.

In contrast, katabatic winds blow offshore, and because of this they can be very dangerous to any small boat. These winds occur when cold air accumulates on snow-covered hills and mountains. The pressure builds up and any small change in atmospheric conditions releases this dammed up air, causing it to rush down the mountain slopes and out to sea. In the Aleutian Islands these winds are called williwaws, and it was these horrifying avalanches of cold air that caused a whole race of people to build their homes underground.

High coasts and cliff-lined shores bring their own problems, and what appear to be safe onshore winds can be deflected to blow parallel to the coast. You can also expect sudden wind shifts near islands and headlands.

Because wind is the ocean kayaker's greatest enemy, a knowledge of the Beaufort Wind Scale is essential if any weather forecast you hear is to be interpreted correctly. This scale normally gives the Beaufort number, the speed range of the wind in knots, a description of the wind, the condition of the sea, and the probable height of the waves in meters. The wind direction indicates the compass quarter from which the wind is expected (e.g., a northerly wind blows from the north).

The Beaufort Wind Scale applies only to open water, and you may be paddling with a fetch of only two or three miles. (Fetch is that distance over which the wind blows unhindered.) The sea state in that case might be almost flat, even with a Force 8 gale. Therefore, to be of more use to the paddler, I have given a table based on the formula for kinetic energy by which to make comparisons. You may be misguided into thinking that because you can cope with a

Force 5 wind, you can also cope with a Force 6 wind—after all, it is only one unit up the Beaufort Wind Scale. The difference is considerable, however, and the pressure on the chest of the paddler if going into the wind is 220 units for Force 5 to 364 units during a Force 6. On my Beaufort Wind Scale, therefore, I have included a column for the energy or wind pressure that shows the energy ratio of the wind or, more precisely, the pressure of the wind against the body of the paddler and kayak.

Fog. The most common type of fog is known as advection fog. It is caused by relatively warm air blowing over a cold sea, usually during the spring or summer months. Fogs such as this are often associated with cold currents like the Labrador and California currents. Unfortunately for the sea paddler, winds do not tend to decrease during these fogs, but in fact remain quite strong. Advection fog is different from radiation fog, which forms over land masses on cold windless nights and can extend ten to fifteen miles offshore. Radiation fog is usually dispersed by the heat of the morning sun.

It is important that you know the names of the different audible fog signals and be able to differentiate between them. It is not much good if you do not know whether the wailing you can hear through the fog is a typhon or a diaphone, especially if the chart tells you that the two signals are ten miles apart!

When training advanced groups in fog, and the shore is invisible, have some well-qualified helpers with you. Every member of the group should carry a compass and a whistle or a hand-held fog horn. In case of emergency, each should have a compass bearing that will get him back to shore again. It is best if the leader carries a loud audible signal that his group can "home in" on.

Do not practice fog navigation in shipping channels. If you wish to keep shipping well clear of you and your group in an emergency, sound a "D" in morse (i.e., one long blast followed by two short ones) and repeat this three times, then a two-minute pause and keep repeating. This signal will keep shipping clear of you if they are small enough to maneuver. But please note, it is not a distress signal.

Audible Fog Signals:

Diaphone—(dia.) This is a powerful low pitch sound finishing with a deep grunt.

Siren—There are various types of sirens having different strengths and pitches.

Reed—This gives a feeble rather high-pitched note.

Typhon—A strong medium-pitched note that sounds like a ship's fog signal.

Horn—Some wail, some give off sounds of different pitches combined together, others give a long steady tone while some seem to waver up and down. These sounds are very distinctive and once heard are easily remembered.

Whistle—(whis.) These are often worked by the swaying of the buoy. They can be shrill and clear, but if the swell is erratic the whistle will start and finish with a wheezing gasp.

Bells—Bells go ping, gongs go bong—some even go clonk—but you will be surprised just how far their sounds can carry.

The best way to learn about fog is to do a lot of exploring close to home.

Take time to familiarize yourself with your local sea area, especially in the area where most of your paddling takes place. There is no substitute for local knowledge. Get used to the sound, sight, and position of all the local buoys and especially the fog signals. Each of these signals usually has a sound or frequency different from nearby fog signals. One of the best illustrations of this is in the San Francisco Bay area. The bay is often shrouded in fog, and in the immediate vicinity of the Golden Gate Bridge there are about eight audible and assorted fog signals, which to the uninitiated ear can be very confusing.

Carry a compass and get used to the position of all local horns, whistles, sirens, and diaphones. Carry some audible means of signaling your own position in case there is a danger of some less prudent water user colliding with your kayak. A whistle is adequate, but a fog horn is better. If all the members of a group have such signals, it becomes an easy matter to keep in contact with one another.

Cultivate a good sense of hearing. Take time to stop paddling and sit quietly and listen to the sounds, which are indications of land. Perhaps a dog is barking or there is the sound of surf rumbling upon rocks. From faraway comes the sound of distant traffic or nearby is the sound of the engines of a large vessel. Whatever the sounds, become aware of them and what they tell you about what is happening in your immediate vicinity. With practice the compass can be disregarded and fog navigation can become a matter of experience and instinct in local waters.

During times of poor visibility paddlers should maintain good group discipline and keep within communication distance of one another. Be careful especially close inshore on rocky coasts.

HAZARDOUS WILDLIFE

Many areas of the world have their own particular dangers. In this chapter I shall deal with only a small number in the hope they will inspire the would-be gypsy paddler into doing thorough research before departing for strange or inhospitable coastlines.

It will soon become apparent to you that there are any number of God's creatures just waiting to suck your blood, bite or sting you, and even eat you and your supplies. A number of examples come immediately to mind. Eskimo sledge dogs have been known to eat camera cases with the film, boots, and straps. Porcupines love salt and will devour any wooden paddles left lying about that are impregnated with it. Mice will eat their way through plastic bags to get at a food supply. While on the Aleutian Islands, we had either rats or squirrels (we never found out which) eat their way through a spray cover, then through a tent bag with tent before helping themselves to our dehydrated food. The tent had to be repaired and the food reallocated, so even small animals can create big problems.

Mosquitoes

If paddling takes you to the Arctic tundra, your life can be ruled by a tiny humming insect. The mosquito is most active during the time you spend on land and not paddling—i.e., early morning and evening. These pests are at best unpleasant, but when they are present in large numbers they can be completely insufferable. Visibility is impaired by thick, impenetrable swarms. They can stampede a herd of caribou and drive men just about mad. Eating is a misery and, what is more, they can bite through quite thick clothing.

It will easily be understood that from his constrained position in the kaiak, which does not permit of much turning, the hunter cannot throw backwards or to the right. If, then, a wounded seal suddenly attacks him from these quarters, it requires both skill and presence of mind to elude it or to turn so quickly as to aim a fatal throw at it before it has time to do him damage. It is just as bad when he is attacked from below, or when the animal suddenly shoots up close at his side, for it is lightning-like in its movements and lacks neither courage nor strength. If it once gets up on the kaiak and capsizes it, there is little hope of rescue. It will often attack the hunter under water, or throw itself upon the bottom of the kaiak and tear holes in it. In such a predicament, it needs very unusual self-mastery to preserve the coolness necessary for recovering oneself upon even keel and renewing the fight with the furious adversary. And yet it sometimes happens that after being thus capsized the kaiak-man brings the seal home in triumph. (Nansen, Eskimo Life, pp., 73–74.)

There are ways of keeping this menace at bay. If you know that mosquitoes are going to be a problem, make sure that your tent has netting at the vents as well as the door. If there is plenty of ventilation inside the tent, burn an antimosquito coil. The fumes from this are supposed to repel even the hardiest insect. You can, of course, smear your skin with any of the local special repellents, and there is even a tiny battery-operated device, which emits the high-pitched whistle of the male mosquito and is supposed to scare away the pregnant female—the one that does the biting. Every member of the group should have a head net. These are usually sold at stores and sports shops in mosquito areas. Thin cotton shirts are useless for protection. Treat mosquito bites by washing with cold, clear water and then bathing with calamine lotion.

Ticks

These are unpleasant little creatures that burrow into the flesh. Once dug in, only their rear ends stick out. There are a number of ways to withdraw these darlings. Use a suction cup (same as for a bee sting) or touch the tick with the hot end of a piece of wire or a blown-out match.

It is possible to remove ticks with long, fine-jawed tweezers, but take care not to leave the head behind, as the wound could become infected. Grasp the tick's head as close to the skin as possible and gently pull it straight out. Be careful not to squeeze the tick's body, as this may cause it to inject its fluid into you. Afterward, wash the bite area with antiseptic.

Someone once recommended touching a hot cigarette end to a tick, so I tried this on a harmless species that I had found busily burrowing into my stomach. It was not the best advice, because my skin started to sizzle before the hot end of the cigarette got anywhere near the back end of the tick.

Some North American ticks can be dangerous as well as unpleasant. The bite of a deer tick can inflict a bacterial infection known as Lyme disease. These little fellows are found in all types of vegetation and on animals, especially in the woods. Deer ticks are most active in the autumn and spring but are also present throughout the summer.

The disease has obvious symptoms. Within four to twenty days a ring-shaped rash may occur. The symptoms may also include fever, chills, headache,

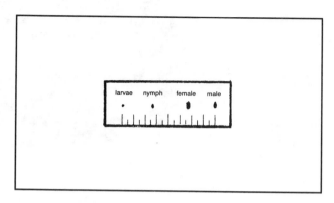

86. Actual size of Deer Tick compared to one inch.

weakness and fatigue, and stiffness in the joints. In some cases there are no symptoms, while some common symptoms of Lyme disease may mimic arthritis. If you think that you have been bitten and have the symptoms, contact your doctor. If detected early, Lyme disease is usually treatable with antibiotics.

Recognize which tick is dangerous (fig. 86). You are looking for something tiny—about one-sixteenth inch wide—and orange-brown with a black spot near the head. The wood tick, which has white marks near its head, is about twice as big as a deer tick and is unlikely to give you Lyme disease.

Take precautions when camping in infested areas. Wear long sleeves and long pants tucked into socks. Use an insect repellent and check your body constantly; get someone else to check your back. Brush off your clothing before going into your tent.

Jellyfish

As a general rule most of the large, colorful jellyfish will give you a sting, and so will some of the smaller ones. Jellyfish have a histamine sting that causes irritation and burning at the point of contact. You will feel as if your skin has been beaten with stinging nettles.

Some people are allergic to histamine stings, and if this is the case, there may be a tightness in the victim's chest during the few hours after contact. The victim may have difficulty breathing and may even faint and collapse. If this happens, you need a doctor as soon as possible.

Prevention is better than cure, of course, and you should give all colorful jellyfish a wide berth whether they are floating or stranded on the beach, whole or in bits.

If the worst has happened, wipe away any part of the jellyfish still clinging to the skin, but *not with your hands.* Use sand or salt water. Apply an antihistamine or hydrocortisone cream or lotion. If you are on a surfing beach, a bystander or one of your companions may have some antihistamine tablets for hay fever for use if the patient's respiration becomes difficult.

Portuguese Man-of-War.　The Portuguese man-of-war (also known as the Blue Bottle) is dealt with separately because it is certainly in a class of its own (fig. 87). Unlike most jellyfish, it is not just unpleasant, it is a killer. Because of this it is well that you know something about it and are able to recognize it on sight.

It moves across the surface of the sea by means of a gas-filled bladder, which is blown by the wind, and it looks like a sail. The bladder is not large (it is about six inches long) and is pale blue in color with a touch of pink. From this float a complicated system of tentacles hang down to a length of more than forty-five feet, and each of these tentacles is equipped along the whole of its length with row upon row of minute barbed, flexible hypodermic syringes. Each one of these can inject a highly toxic poison. As these long fronds hang limply down in the water, all the tiny barbs are coiled up ready and waiting for the unsuspecting touch of a victim. The moment these tentacles are brushed against, the harpoons shoot out and cling with horrifying results.

To get some idea of the Portuguese man-of-war's power, I spoke to a young man whose legs had become entangled in the tentacles while swimming. He described the agonizing pain he suffered as like having red hot wires wrapped around his legs. He spent nearly six months in a hospital, and at one time it was thought that his legs might have to be amputated. Years after, the evidence is there for all to see in the form of scar tissue that spirals around his legs from his ankles to the top of his thighs.

To treat Portuguese man-of-war stings, first rinse the affected area with methylated spirit. Then with great care remove any stinging tentacles that may still be adhering to the skin. Do not touch them with your bare hands. After you have done this, rinse the area again with methylated spirits.

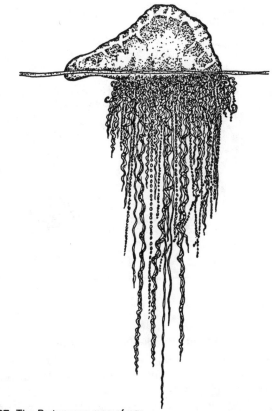

87. The Portuguese man-of-war.

If the sting area is extensive, you will need medical help as quickly as possible. Meanwhile, treat the sufferer for shock. There may be respiratory difficulties or failure followed by cardiac arrest, in which case administer mouth-to-mouth resuscitation and massage the heart. The patient may also need pain-killing tablets.

Sea Wasp.　The sea wasp is a truly deadly inhabitant of the sea, and because of its translucence it is difficult to see (fig. 88). Normally the bell of this jellyfish is not large, only about eight inches high. The four clumps of tentacles that hang down, however, can be several yards long. Some specimens are known to have grown much larger.

The sting from this creature is extremely venomous, and if you are severely stung your life expectancy could be measured in minutes rather than hours. Even a sting covering a very small area is excruciatingly painful, and the effects can last for ten hours or more.

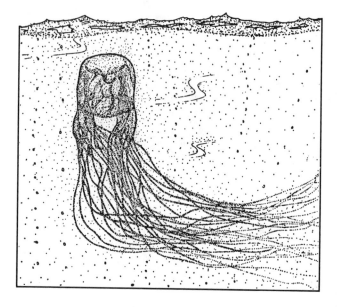

88. The sea wasp.

The severity of the sting is in direct proportion to the size of the animal, and swimmers have been known to swallow tiny ones accidentally without any lasting harmful effects. Luckily for most of us, this horror only affects those who kayak in certain parts of the Pacific Ocean and the northeast coast of Australia. It has been discovered that ladies' pantyhose provide very good protection, and I am told that quite a number of Australian lifeguards protect their legs in this way.

If you or someone else is stung, get medical assistance immediately. It has been found that applying vinegar gives relief from the pain. Give pain-killing tablets and treat for shock. If no vinegar is available, wash the affected parts with cold, clean water.

Snakes

I shall not include what to do if you are being slowly swallowed by a boa constrictor; however, there are thirty thousand deaths every year from snake bites, so I feel some information is worth including in this book. In the case of snake bites, the outlook is always good and most people recover completely except for cases in which the victim is bitten numerous times, has unusual sensitivity to snake poison, or is bitten near the heart; cases when there is undue de-

lay or when no action is taken; and cases involving very old or very young people.

In Britain the snake problem hardly exists at all. The only poisonous snake that has its home in the British Isles is the adder, and you will see it only if your paddles take you to the more remote parts of Scotland or the Western Isles.

In North America there are a number of snakes you should be familiar with: coral snake, rattlesnake, cottonmouth (or water moccasin), and copperhead.

Prevention of snake bites is far better than cure, and there are some precautions that can be taken to minimize the risk of being bitten. Look where you are going when in snake country, and do not go prancing about in bare feet. Better still, wear boots—the higher the better. Snow gaiters might be handy in this situation. When you are looking for wood, poke about with a long stick first and take care when you are lifting flat stones for the hearth or wandering through long grass. When paddling through swamps, look out for low branches and do not dabble your hands in the water while you are resting.

If you are bitten, remember the following:
- Do not panic—keep calm and do not run for help.
- Kill the snake with a rock or your heel and keep it for identification. It may be needed afterward so that the right kind of serum can be administered.
- Apply a suction cup over the bite to draw out the poison. Fill a small glass bottle with hot water. Then empty out the water and place the neck of the bottle over the bite. As the bottle cools, the vacuum formed inside sucks the poison out of the bite.
- While this is going on, you need to know whether the snake that bit you is poisonous. Wash the blood away and check the wound carefully. Squeeze it to make the blood ooze out. If the blood shows from a number of small punctures arranged in a semicircle, then the bite probably is not poisonous. If, however, there are only two punctures, these are fang marks and more than likely you have been bitten by a venomous snake. Unfortunately, a weak bite from a nonpoisonous snake may leave only two puncture marks, and a hard bite from a poisonous one may leave several marks.

- You may have to apply a tourniquet, which should be loosened every twenty minutes for one minute. The patient should be observed closely, especially during this one-minute period.
- Keep the patient immobile and wash the wound with soap and water.
- Keep ice or cold water on the wound; this will reduce the speed at which the poison is absorbed into the bloodstream and also will reduce the pain.
- Treat the patient as for a fever. Keep the patient warm so that he perspires; this will get rid of body wastes and reduce the fever.
- If no medical help is immediately forthcoming, an adult should be given four tablets oral penicillin (if no allergy) plus four capsules twenty-five milligrams of Benadryl. Repeat two penicillin tablets every four hours.

How long it is before complications set in depends very much on how serious the bite is—how near to the heart, the age of the patient, and the amount of venom. With the bite from a pit viper, which includes the rattlesnake, cottonmouth, and copperhead, you have from half an hour to about four hours.

Bears

North America offers some wonderful coastline for ocean kayaking, and the coast of Alaska is the most beautiful I have ever seen. If, however, you choose to paddle along some of these coastal wildernesses, then very often you must be prepared to share this beauty with a very large animal. Its name is the brown bear, and although this great beast normally is quite happy eating berries, if it is surprised or provoked it will be equally happy to eat you.

Three types of bear inhabit North America: the comparatively small and quite numerous black bear, the polar bear, and the brown or grizzly bear. Actually the grizzly lives well inland and is smaller than the coastal brown bear, which can grow to a staggering twelve hundred pounds.

The brown bear, silvertips, or grizzlies—call them what you will—are really in a class by themselves. They are the world's largest land carnivores and, furthermore, they can run at speeds of up to thirty miles per hour. Bears are shy and would sooner

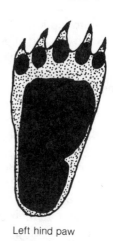

Left hind paw

Left forepaw

89. Brown bear tracks.

avoid you if they are given the chance. They no more desire to bump into you than you desire to bump into them, but they do hate being surprised.

During the summer months, polar bears tend to move northward with the ice floes. Like the brown bear, these animals are highly dangerous killers and should be given a wide berth. Because polar bears exist where there are no trees to impede their line of sight, I would say that if you can see one with the naked eye and you are not paddling, then you are too close because they will also have you picked out.

Signs of Bear Activity. Bears have five toes with long claws on each foot (see fig. 89). They tread mainly on the front part of the forefoot so it is only on clear tracks in soft earth that you will see the complete sole. The size of the forefoot track depends on the age of the bear, but in a fully grown specimen it will be about eight inches wide and approximately eleven inches long. The hind foot makes a print rather like that of a barefoot man, except that on a bear the big toe is the shortest and smallest. The hind track of a fully grown brown bear is approximately six inches wide and twelve inches long. When a bear is walking normally, the hind foot is placed a good distance in front of the forefoot track.

Brown bear droppings are cylindrical in shape and about six inches thick. During the summer months they are found in large piles and consist of fur, bits of bone, and the remains of plants. When berry time comes around in the autumn, the feces are soft or liquid. When landing at dusk, it is a good thing to be able to identify bear droppings, especially fresh ones.

Precautions in Bear Country. Here are some ways to minimize a confrontation with a bear when you are forced to make camp in bear country:

- Do not pitch your tent too near a bear run. Look for long lines of footprints or flattened grass.
- Do not take shortcuts through alder bushes—bears love alder.
- Do not camp too near the mouths of salmon streams, especially if there are a lot of half-eaten salmon about. Look out for bear signs such as droppings or footprints.
- Never pass between a sow and her cub. If when you land you stumble upon a cuddly cub that looks all lonely and friendless, mummy will not be far away, so get back into your kayak and leave—in a hurry!
- Do not take strolls during the hours of darkness.
- Bears associate humans with food. Do not attract them by keeping a dirty and sloppy campsite.
- Do not leave foodstuffs around the campsite and do any cooking well away from the tents.
- Do not eat or store any food in your tent (including gum or chocolate).
- Store any foodstuffs out of reach. Substances that have a fairly neutral smell, such as freeze-dried and dehydrated foods that are packed in plastic, can be kept in the sealed watertight compartments of kayaks. Any other food should be bagged and hung high in the air on a line slung between two trees. (I have known a bear to tear off a spray cover to get a chocolate that was left in the cockpit while totally ignoring food stored elsewhere in the kayak.)
- Make plenty of noise when you land—talk loudly, whistle, sing, or bang the deck of your kayak. If you must wander about in bear country, try to let the animals know you are coming. Some people suggest bells fastened to clothing, others advocate rattling small stones inside tins.
- At night, keep a flare inside your tent; this might help scare away any bear who becomes too inquisitive.
- Mark the boundaries of your territory, even if it is only a one-night stop. Most animals do this, and the method is simple. Just urinate where any tracks lead to your campsite or at any gaps in the foliage where you think an animal might wander in. If signs of bear abound, as an added precaution you could urinate around your tent.

If the worst happens—and it might—there are no signs that indicate if a bear is about to charge. In the case of a close encounter, quietly talking while slowly backing away has been known to work. As you move, try to get out of the bear's line of sight behind a tree or boulder. If you are trying to escape a brown bear and there is a tree nearby that can be climbed, climb it quickly because the bear will not be able to follow you. The smaller black bear, however, can climb trees and will follow you up. If the bear charges and you have no way of defending yourself (and you certainly will not outrun a bear), I am told the best way to escape death or a bad mauling is to feign death. Lie on the ground and curl up into a ball with knees up and hands clasped behind your neck. Bears kill by biting the back of the neck or the throat, or by disemboweling; however I am told that if you can lie still and suffer the first few blows and bites without screaming out, the bear may consider you no longer a threat and leave you alone.

An old trapper once said to me, "The guy who goes out into the bush without the means of getting his dinner or defending himself is nuts!" Considering this, it would be prudent to carry a suitable firearm when in bear country. However, it has occurred to me that a small orange distress smoke canister set off at the right time might enable a dignified retreat to take place without any blood being shed on either side.

Alligators

A story that appeared in *Canoe* magazine tells of how on one December day, about seven miles north of Florida's Silver Springs boat ramps, a competitive paddler named Dave Phillips found to his delight that he was leading the Oklawaha River Kayak Race. At a point where the river is about sixty feet wide, he saw an alligator on the surface right in the center of the river. The alligator, which appeared to be eight to ten feet long, turned and began to swim toward him. About twenty feet from the paddler, hissing and grunting, the gator opened its jaws wide. Dave, who was still approaching at about seven mph, shouted at the beast in an attempt to scare it off.

He then tried to turn the kayak away by twisting his body so that the hull would be presented to the gator, which by this time was attempting to snap at him in the cockpit. As it did so, he capsized and came out on the side away from the gator's jaws, which were sliding along the fiberglass hull. Phillips's thirty-foot swim to shore was accomplished in record time. By now the gator had released the kayak and was floating alongside it. As the next competitors approached, the gator submerged.

The incident ended without bloodshed on either side. Phillips, much shaken, retrieved his boat, patched it up with duct tape, and paddled on to finish second. The gator had left its mark, however; its jaws had crushed a part of the top deck and put a number of tooth holes in the hull.

As no one was hurt, this incident was not considered an attack. A Fish and Game officer later apologized for the alligator, saying that it probably mistook Phillips for a seventeen-foot-long, yellow-and-white swimming deer!

The best way to explore the waterways of Florida is undoubtedly by sea kayak. However, there are a million alligators in the state. They are protected by law, and their numbers are increasing. Since alligators *do* eat people, it is important to observe a few simple precautions in areas where alligators are known to live.

- Exercise extreme caution when landing. Alligators blend into the background so as to be almost invisible.
- Camp only on the raised platforms provided by the park service; otherwise sleep in a tree! Bear in mind that alligators feed at dusk and at night.
- Do not tease them or throw food to them.
- Beware of the seemingly harmless small baby alligators. They have a nasty bite, and mother is probably nearby looking for the next meal.
- Do not imitate the alligator's *ugh, ugh, ugh* sound when in their presence. This is the sound made by an alligator in distress, and it encourages all other adult alligators to come to its assistance.

Sharks

All predators need to protect themselves from any damage that would disable them or limit their efficiency. It is for this reason that sharks close their eyes as they open their mouths to bite. It may also explain why, over the years, divers have found that a sharp blow inflicted anywhere on a shark's body, but especially on its snout, is enough to make it think twice about making an attack. If a kayak paddler is to benefit from this knowledge, he needs some implement that can deliver an immediate blow to an inquisitive shark, but that is also portable and can be wielded safely from the cockpit of his kayak.

A bang stick (fig. 23) has the disadvantage of being highly specialized. It is not easy to inflict a positive hit with the first attempt. A glancing blow, which is no deterrent, is more likely, and the kayaker can then find himself in a more dangerous position. Because the bang stick is itself a potentially dangerous piece of equipment, it will need to be put on and taken off the deck before and after every trip. When the big moment arrives, the bang stick may well prove to be a rusty relic or even to have been forgotten altogether.

What is needed is an implement that can be carried as part of the kayak's permanent equipment and that preferably could lie alongside the spare paddle. After consulting with sport fishermen and others who have come into unwelcome contact with sharks, I offer the following suggestion, which I have called the panic prod.

In its simplest form, it consists of a piece of hardwood, round in section, about one and a half to two inches in diameter, and about three feet long. It has a loose shock-cord wrist loop at one end and a three-inch spike at the other. The spike is a simple non-barbed type to allow the fish to pull free from the prod as it swims past. The paddler is therefore at considerably less risk of unwillingly accompanying the shark. Although not the perfect answer to a frightening problem, the panic prod is based on the well-known principal of "any port in a storm," and I feel sure it might well give paddlers a means of escape from all but the most determined of shark attacks.

EMERGENCY AID

Cramp

Cramp is a very painful condition caused by the sudden and agonizing contraction of a muscle or group of muscles. It can stop you walking, paddling, swimming, or even breathing, depending on which muscles are affected. If you are in the wrong place when you get an attack of cramp, you could even finish up dead.

This sudden muscle contraction can be brought about in a number of ways:

- By exertion and chilling from wind and water.
- By keeping a limb immobile in an unnatural or unusual position.
- By a poor sitting or footrest position. With novices, cramp is often caused by undue anxiety and tension (group leaders take note).
- By a salt deficiency in the bloodstream.

Relief from cramp can be obtained only by straightening and exercising the affected limbs. If the cramp affects the lower part of a paddler's body or legs, the patient must raft up between two others and then either stand up, supported by them, or lie along his own reardeck with his feet out of the cockpit. In this way, limbs can be easily flexed and good circulation restored. Whether the victim stands up or lies down depends on how rough the sea is.

If the cramp is persistent, the sufferer should be taken to shore or a capsize may occur—especially if the condition is due to tension.

Tenosynovitis

This is the kayaker's horror, and when it hits there is certainly no mistaking it. There will be a swelling of the forearm, and if you open and close the fingers you will hear a horrifying grating sound, like the creaking of new leather. It also hurts. Place your fingers on the offending spot; it is easy to feel the roughness of the moving tendon.

What has happened is very simple: the overactivity of the flexor tendons at the wrist have caused a swelling inside the tendon sheath. Hence the feeling that the tendon is being gripped by lumpy sandpaper as it moves inside the arm.

This painful condition is caused by unaccustomed activity or prolonged strain, and even experienced kayakers can fall victim to tenosynovitis after a long and grueling paddle, especially if conditions have been unexpectedly severe. Towing someone over a long distance can also cause this, so group leaders should make sure that any towing problem is shared by a number of people, no matter how strong and heroic the volunteers say they are.

The initial treatment for tenosynovitis is simple but drastic for the kayaker. The arm needs rest, so paddling must stop and the arm should be strapped up for one to three weeks. Do not be tempted to paddle in spite of the pain, as this could be dangerous. If the condition is ignored for even a short while, it could take up to three months to cure as well as an operation to free a tendon that may have adhered to its sheath.

If this happens on an expedition, the patient can do no more paddling and will have to be towed back to civilization. However, if the wrist and forearm are put in a splint, it may be possible for the patient to assist the person towing by steering and perhaps paddling a little from time to time.

Fishhooks

Fishhooks can be very nasty, but it might not even be one of your own hooks that does the damage. I have seen a paddler caught on the forehead by a hook that was left hanging from the branch of a tree by some careless fisherman. The hook cannot be extracted the way it went it, so push it forward until the barb breaks back out through the skin (fig. 90A). Cut the hook with pliers or wire cutters either where the hook entered or where it comes out (fig. 90B).

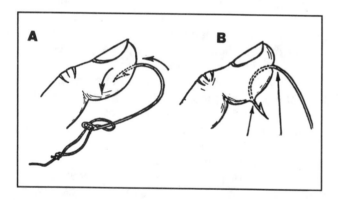

90. Removing a fishhook.

Mouth-to-Mouth Resuscitation

Anyone who needs mouth-to-mouth resuscitation will not look pleasant as they lie upon the sand. The color of their face will be gray or white. The lips and ears will be dark purple, and a yellow froth may be coming from the mouth, together with bits and pieces of their last meal. The time to decide whether you could place your lips against those of this endangered victim is now while you read this book. If you feel that squeamishness would outweigh your humanitarian feelings, then acquaint yourself with one of the manual methods of artificial respiration. However, there are very good reasons why you should fight back nausea and use mouth-to-mouth resuscitation.

The advantages of mouth-to-mouth resuscitation are as follows:

- It can be started sooner than any other method—for instance in the water or across the deck of a kayak.
- Oxygen gets into the victim's lungs quicker than with any of the manual methods.
- The carbon monoxide contained in the rescuer's expired air can trigger the patient's own natural breathing.
- The patient is in the correct position should the rescuer need to administer cardiac massage.
- The rescuer can watch to see if the victim's face changes color and can watch the rise and fall of the chest.
- The rescuer has both hands free and can insure that the victim's airway is clear.
- No special equipment is needed.

To apply mouth-to-mouth resuscitation, first lay the patient flat. If there is time, position his head higher than his stomach. This should keep the fluids in the stomach. If the victim vomits, twist him over onto his side at once; otherwise he will inhale the vomit and choke.

Next, clear the mouth. Put your fingers in and check for dentures, bits of seaweed, or other obstructing material.

Then tilt the patient's head back. This should be twisted back as far as it will go, so that the chin sticks out (fig. 91A).

Make an airtight seal. This is done by opening your mouth wide enough to make a seal over the victim's nose and then blowing (fig. 91B). Use the hand that is supporting the chin to keep the victim's lips together.

If the nose is blocked, use the hand that is supporting the chin to open the victim's mouth. Open your mouth wide and make a seal over his mouth, then blow. If some air escapes from the victim's nose, either pinch his nostrils together or press your cheek against his nose. As you blow, watch out of the corner of your eye to see if his chest rises.

After you have blown into the patient's mouth, turn your head away and allow the air inside his lungs

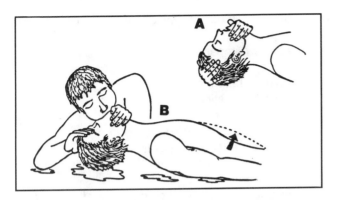

91. Mouth-to-mouth resuscitation.

to escape. At the same time you can observe his chest go down. Start resuscitation with four to five quick inflations, then blow in time with your own breathing (twelve to fifteen times a minute).

All being well, the patient's color should soon look more healthy—he should have red lips and pink cheeks. You must continue with mouth-to-mouth resuscitation until he is breathing on his own again—no matter how long this takes—or until a doctor tells you to stop. When the patient recovers, treat for shock.

There are several reasons for using mouth-to-nose instead of mouth-to-mouth resuscitation. It reduces the risk of air entering the stomach because the nose reduces and directs the air that otherwise would be forced into the stomach. This means there is less possibility of vomiting, so it is ideal for drowning cases. It is easier to make an airtight seal over the nose with the mouth. There might, however, be problems if the victim has a history of sinus trouble or has a cold.

If by some mischance the patient's chest does not rise when his head is bent right back and his mouth is clear, you have a stoppage. Very quickly, turn the patient over onto his face with his arms above his head. Place your feet astride his waist and lift him, then move your feet together so that he is trapped between your knees. Pull his head back, by the hair if necessary. This will give you a straight airway. Give him a hard pushing blow two or three times between the shoulder blades. This should dislodge any obstruction and enable you to continue with mouth-to-mouth resuscitation.

If the victim's stomach rises up while you are administering mouth-to-mouth resuscitation, this is a sign that air has found its way inside. You must press on the air bulge gently but firmly so the wind comes out. This will probably cause the patient to vomit, in which case turn him over so that his head is on one side.

Dangers of Fresh Water. With mouth-to-mouth resuscitation every second is vital. However, the urgency is greater when fresh water is involved. Any fresh water that gets into the lungs is absorbed into the bloodstream very quickly. This will dilute the blood and affect the heart rapidly. Salt water, on the other hand, is not absorbed into the blood at all, which means that the heart is not affected so quickly.

As a general rule, in fresh water a victim is thought to be beyond help after being immersed for three minutes, whereas with salt water there is hope of resuscitation even after the victim has been submerged for as long as five minutes.

Raft-Assisted Resuscitation. Using kayaks rafted together, mouth-to-mouth resuscitation can be carried out as easily on water as on land (fig. 92). Probably the best way to go about this is for the rescuer in the boat nearest the victim to turn round so that he is turning in toward the raft. The man in the boat farthest away from the unconscious person then reaches across his partner's kayak, grabs the victim's wrists, and with a concentrated heave pulls him over and across the raft. The patient is then turned over and mouth-to-mouth resuscitation can begin.

It is possible for the two-man raft to be towed to shore by a third paddler, but in populated areas it would be far more prudent to send up a distress

92. Raft-assisted mouth-to-mouth resuscitation on the water.

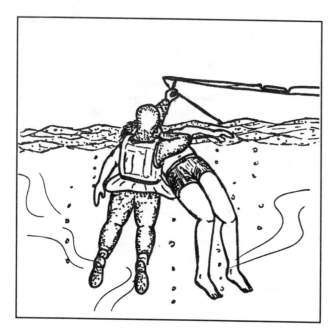

93. Kayak-supported mouth-to-mouth resuscitation in the water.

rocket the moment the unconscious person is sighted. In this way, professional help can be on its way while mouth-to-mouth resuscitation is in progress. Remember that anyone who has been unconscious for any reason should be examined by a doctor as soon as possible.

Kayak-Supported Resuscitation. To perform resuscitation in the water while supported by a kayak (fig. 93) you must first jump out of your boat. Be careful not to capsize it and do not forget to put your paddle in the paddle park. Hold onto the front of your kayak by its lifting toggle. Using this as a support, bend the patient's head well back over your arm. Make sure you keep your hand off his throat and start mouth-to-mouth resuscitation. It is not easy and you will find it awkward and exhausting work.

Shock

How bad the shock is depends on how bad the cause was. Shock usually accompanies injuries, sudden illness, or severe pain.

Shock may be recognized by one or more of the following:

- Your companion may look very white faced.
- His pulse rate becomes faster but weaker.
- He will start to pant with quick, rapid breaths.
- He is sweating but his skin is cold and clammy.
- He may feel sick and vomit.
- He may become very anxious.
- He could complain of thirst.
- He may feel faint and dizzy and complain of blurred vision.

To treat shock you should first of all try to deal with whatever has caused the shock. Then lay the patient down, head low and turned to one side. Raise the legs if possible and loosen all clothing at the neck, chest, and waist. Cover him with a sleeping bag or blanket and reassure him continually. You could moisten his lips with water if he complains of thirst.

Do not heat the victim with hot water bottles or anything else that could drain heat from the inner vital organs.

Do not give the victim anything to drink, and if he is injured, keep him still.

Hypothermia

Hypothermia is the main killer of water users and those who seek recreation out of doors. It is caused by exposure to cold and is aggravated by wet, exhaustion, and wind. To die of cold it is not necessary to be in arctic conditions; most cases occur between thirty and fifty degrees Fahrenheit.

There are many situations that can cause people to become dangerously cold, but there are some that are specific to paddlers. Immersion in cold water is the obvious cause, but the not-so-obvious danger is when a person is being towed. If the kayaker has been paddling hard before needing assistance, his body will be soaked with perspiration and the sudden inactivity will make him vulnerable to the chilling effect of the wind. Once on land, pitching a tent in wind and driving rain when soaked with perspiration is also dangerous.

If you are a leader, think in terms of hypothermia all the time, and just because you feel fine does not mean that your group feels the same. Be aware of the condition of others and the moment you think all is not well, paddle for land, make camp, and light a roaring fire. Disregard people who say they feel fine when the symptoms tell you otherwise.

Cold kills in two stages. The first stage is exposure and exhaustion. The minute you start to lose body heat faster than your body produces it, you are suffering from exposure. To remedy this, you can flap your arms about and jump up and down. Meanwhile, your internal heating system makes involuntary adjustments to preserve the heat to the inner core of vital organs—you shiver. Unfortunately, this will drain your reserves of energy. The only way to stop this drain is to get somewhere away from the cause of your discomfort, put on some dry clothing, and drink something hot.

The second stage is hypothermia. If you are unable to escape from the conditions that are chilling you, your condition will deteriorate until your energy reserves are exhausted and cold starts to affect the brain. At this stage people start to act irrationally and gibber nonsense incessantly. They do not answer questions put to them. This is because the brain has been cooled to such an extent that they lose the power to act and think sensibly. They are now beyond caring and are unable to help themselves. The internal temperature is now dropping fast. Consciousness will come and go. If the condition is not treated, the sufferer will soon lapse into a coma, then very quickly collapse completely and die.

A review of the symptoms and accompanying body temperature is as follows:

- Uncontrollable shivering (ninety-one to ninety-eight degrees Fahrenheit).
- Shivering stops, muscles become rigid, speech is slurred, erratic paddling (ninety to ninety-one degrees Fahrenheit).
- Lapses in memory, incoherent speech, paddling stops. If on land, stumbling and drowsiness. To sleep is to die (eighty-three to eighty-eight degrees Fahrenheit).
- Complete exhaustion, unconsciousness (eighty-three degrees Fahrenheit).
- Death (seventy-seven degrees Fahrenheit).

Treatment for Hypothermia. The treatment for hypothermia will depend on what facilities are at hand. If the patient is only semiconscious, you will need medical help immediately, but while you are waiting, here is what you do:

- Get the patient out of the cold and into warm shelter.

- Put him into a polyethylene exposure bag while others look for a house, erect a tent, build a shelter, dig a snow hole, or whatever else is needed. If you are alone with the victim, you may have to decide whether to continue warming the patient or to leave him in the hope of getting help quickly. The important consideration is just how bad the patient's condition is. If he is very bad, it is better to stay and do all you can. Unfortunately, it is something of a *Catch 22* situation.
- Handle the patient carefully. Carry him with the head lower than the feet. His blood pressure will be low and this will keep the blood circulating to the brain.
- Once out of the wind, gently take his clothes off. Do not massage him.
- If breathing is very shallow or the patient has difficulty breathing, you can assist him with mouth-to-mouth resuscitation. If possible, warm oxygen should be administered with a face mask.
- Start to rewarm the patient using one of the following methods. If you have been lucky enough to find a house with a bath, place the victim into stirred hot water 105 to 112 degrees Fahrenheit—test it with your elbow. Support his legs and arms so they are out of the water. If you heat the limbs, the cold blood will change places with the warm blood from the inner core, causing further cooling at the vital organs. If you find a house without a bath, apply hot towels or blankets (115 degrees Fahrenheit) to the patient's chest, neck, groin, and abdomen. Remember, do not attempt to heat his arms and legs. If you have not found a shelter, get the patient into an exposure bag or tent. Once out of the wind, take his clothes off gently and put him into a sleeping bag. Then get some fit warm person to undress and get into the bag with him. Bear in mind that this is not time for prudery—a life is at stake.

Once the patient starts to perspire, recovery is rapid, usually taking one to two hours. At no time during the treatment should alcohol be given to the patient because this will cause the hot/cold blood exchange between the surface and the inner core, mentioned earlier. However, at any time after the patient becomes semiconscious, hot, sweet drinks can be given. They will do little to heat the inner core, but will work wonders with the patient's morale.

Survival Time in Cold Water

The survival time of a poorly clothed person in cold water varies according to a number of factors and different circumstances, but the numbers in figure 94 can be taken as a general rule.

Survival and the Inner Man

Strange things happen when things go wrong. At the moment of fear or stress, a phase of mental and physical activity is triggered off and the body is alerted by a sudden release of adrenaline. The blood pressure and the heart rate increase and the liver sends an increased amount of sugar into the bloodstream. The blood vessels to the skin are restricted, allowing more blood to go to the muscles, which makes them more easily stimulated and less easily tired. It reduces heat loss and increases mental activity. Put all these factors together and you either have the formula for survival or panic.

How a person feels within himself has a great deal to do with his ability to survive. A person who thinks he is beaten usually is. It is the will to survive, that indomitable spirit deep within, which helps man to conquer. To some, fear brings unexpected strength. Others become so weak that gripping a paddle shaft is more than they can manage. Anxiety, doubt, fear, apprehension, and despair are all nails in the coffin of survival. But knowledge dispels fear, and practice in realistic but controlled conditions makes an accident less to be feared when it happens.

Water Surface Temperature		Time of Immersion for Survival
Centigrade	Fahrenheit	
0	32	15 minutes or less.
2.5	36.5	30 minutes.
5	41	1 hour.
10	50	3 hours.
15	59	7 hours.

94. Survival times in cold water.

Calling a Halt to a Trip

Kayak trips may last a couple of days or several weeks, but illness and injuries do not respect people and their plans. It may be necessary at some stage of a trip to call the whole thing off and seek assistance. To help make that decision, if any members of the group complain of the following symptoms, the time is right to call a halt:

- Any bleeding that will not stop.
- Any diarrhea that will not stop.
- Vomiting that does not respond to treatment.
- Severe chest pains that are persistent.
- Any kind of paralysis.
- A persistent fever.
- Severe and persistent stomach pains.
- Shortness of breath or difficultly in breathing.
- Inability to pass urine.
- Any persistent disturbance of speech or vision or any mental disorder.
- Serious bite or sting—for example, scorpion, spider, or poisonous snake.
- Any blow to the head that has caused a loss of consciousness.

STRATEGIES FOR SURVIVAL

During any expedition along wild and unpopulated coastlines it must be accepted that at some stage it may be necessary, due to injury or illness, to abort the trip. You may have to leave kayaks behind and make a journey over inhospitable country in order to save yourself or to get help for others. Group leaders should make sure that anyone they send to get help is fully equipped and has adequate food and water with them.

Some of the following hints are included to prepare the kayaker for just such an emergency.

Water and Thirst

Water that has been filtered through rocks or comes from deep springs is usually fit to drink, but beware of slow-moving streams; no matter how fresh it looks, the rotting body of a fox or other animal may be lying in the water only a few hundred yards upstream from where you are drinking.

If there is any doubt about the purity of water, treat it with water purification tablets, use about five drops of domestic bleach to a pint of water, or just boil it.

If you have had to leave your kayak and travel across hot desert country, it is always best to travel at night when it is cool. In that way you lose far less moisture from your body. If you must walk under the hot sun, keep your body covered and your sleeves down, so your body fluids will be retained longer. Do not walk any distance in hot weather while wearing a wet suit;

people have been known to collapse and die from heat exhaustion doing just that. It is never a good idea to ration water. You will last longer if you drink your fill rather than taking small sips over a long period.

Remember, even in cold conditions paddling a kayak a long way fast can cause you to perspire excessively, which in turn can cause your body to dehydrate. Therefore, regulate your paddling speed over long distances.

Drinking melted snow without boiling it first can cause diarrhea. Pack ice is composed of salt water, but any floating ice that has come from a glacier was once snow, so it should be fresh water—even if the snow did fall at the time of the Crusades!

Salt Water. You can cook in it, boil in it, wash in it, or swim in it, but never drink it. However, the presence of salt water can often help you to find fresh water in a place you would never think of looking.

When the tide is at its lowest, locate the high water mark and dig a few holes on either side of it. You may come to water, and because fresh water is lighter than salt water, it will float on the top. There might only be a thin layer, so suck it out with some tubing or a piece of hollow grass. It might even be possible to rig something up to the kayak's bilge pump, although I have not tried this. The water you extract will be rather murky, but it is not salty and will certainly be better than nothing.

The Solar Still. The solar still produces fresh water. Dig a hole and line it with a clear polyethylene sheet (fig. 95). Any foul water may be placed in hollows

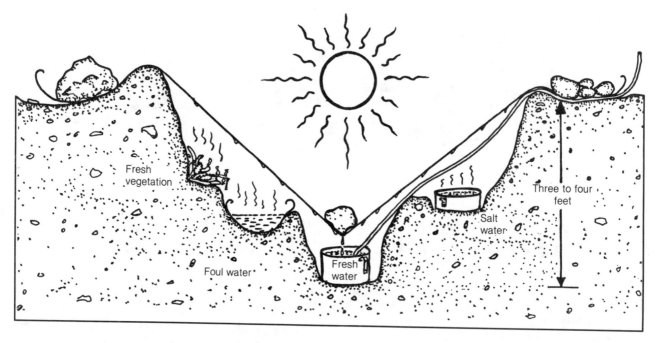

95. A solar still will produce one to three pints of fresh water per day.

lined with smaller pieces of polyethylene. The sun evaporates the foul water and the moisture from the fresh vegetation. This condenses when it touches the clean plastic sheet and the droplets run down into the container at the bottom. Use a tube to retrieve the fresh water, because if you move the sheeting, the whole process will have to start again.

Fire

The importance of a fire cannot be overestimated. It is not just a means of cooking, it is the focal point of any campsite. It is a social center where clothes and equipment can be dried, cold bodies warmed, and chilled spirits raised. Things never appear so desperate if discussed around the hot, bright flame of a wood fire.

When you are trying to light a fire, there is no point in trying to be a purist. Carry tablets to light the fire with you, well sealed and away from your food. Carry both ordinary and windproof/waterproof matches. Spread them around into different packs so that no matter how wet things get, there will always be some dry matches somewhere. If you do not carry

fire lighters, keep a good supply of kindling with you such as dried moss, charred cloth, or the thin paper-like surface of birch bark, which burns well even when wet. Keep fires away and downwind from the tents.

Lighting a Fire by Friction.   Lighting a fire without a match is a soul-destroying job, but you never know just how badly a fire may be needed. Of all the methods I have seen demonstrated, the following North American Indian method is the best (see fig. 96).

Place the fireboard with the notch on the tinder. Kneel and steady the fireboard with your foot. Hold the spindle revolving with long strokes. Keep increasing the pressure. Do not give up until the smoke rises. Blow gently, then knock the hot ember that has been formed into the tinder. Blow steadily but gently until a flame begins, then lay some dry, tiny, previously prepared twigs. If ever a skill needed perseverance, this is it. It does work, but it needs practice. The Eskimos used a specially shaped mouthpiece to hold the spindle. Although I have never tried this, it is probably easier and it leaves one hand free to feed the moss or tinder onto the hot ember.

Lighting a Fire with a Camera Lens.   In bright sunlight, it is possible to light a fire using a camera lens. The wider you can open the lens the

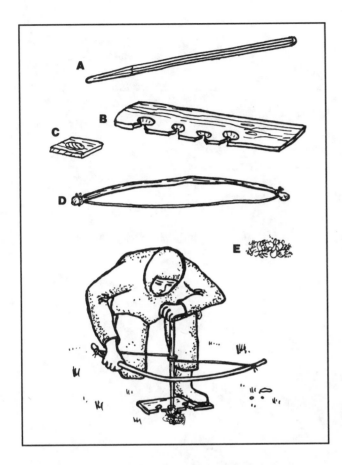

96. Lighting a fire by friction.
Tools for starting a fire by friction consist of: an octagonal spindle approximately one foot long and three-fourths inch thick (A); a fireboard approximately four inches wide, one-half inch thick, and one foot long with hollows and V-shaped cuts for the spindle (B); a wooden handpiece to rest on top of the spindle (C); a bow approximately two feet long with a leather thong or bootlace (D); and extra tinder (moss, shredded bark, wood shavings) to be drying out for the next fire (E).

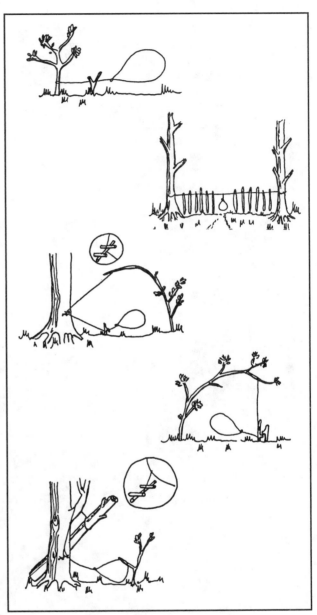

97. Methods of setting snares.

more heat will be produced. Open the back of the camera and hold its open back toward the sun. Focus the sunlight so that it appears on the kindling material—moss or cotton wool—as a bright, white point of light. Get a red ember and blow gently but steadily; then lay on some predried tiny twigs.

With some kinds of eyeglasses (those from a far-sighted person) it is possible to concentrate enough heat to start a flame, but the sunlight must focus to a point to generate enough heat.

Snares

When you carry wire and twine in your repair kit and there is small game about, you will always have the means of filling the cooking pot. Setting snares can take some ingenuity, but the accompanying illustration gives some ideas (fig. 97).

It is a gallant business, this kaiak-hunting; it is like a sportive dance with the sea and with death. There is no finer sight possible than to see the kaiak-man breasting the heavy rollers that seem utterly to engulf him. Or when, over-taken by a storm at sea, the kaiaks run for the shore, they come like black storm-birds rushing before the wind and the waves, which, like roll-ing mountains, sweep on in their wake. The paddles whirl through the air and water, the body is bent a little forwards, the head often turned half backwards to watch the seas; all is life and spirit—while the sea around reeks like a seething cauldron. And then it may happen that when the game is at its wildest a seal pops its head up before them. Quicker than thought the harpoon is seized and rushes through the foam with deadly aim; the seal dashes away with the bladder behind it, but is presently caught and killed, and then towed onwards. Everything is done with the same masterly skill and with the same quiet demeanour. The Eskimo never dreams that he is performing feats of heroism. (Nansen, Eskimo Life, p. 58.)

First find some tracks or flattened grass that will indicate an animal run. Make an easy running loop in the wire. Then, when the snare is set, make sure that the bottom of the loop is not less than a palm's width from the ground.

Fishing

Under normal circumstances, fishing is one of the easiest ways of obtaining a meal when you are out in a coastal wilderness. There are numerous ways of going about this.

Trolling.   Trolling is an ideal method for the kayak paddler. A line is towed behind the boat under the water at a speed of about three miles per hour. Any faster than this and the sinker will plane to the surface together with the hook, defeating the whole object of the exercise. A trolling rig for mackerel and pollack is illustrated in figure 98. The depth of the line behind the kayak is governed by the weight of the lead.

99. An overnight line.

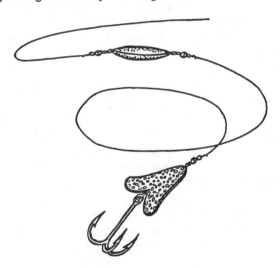

98. A trolling rig for mackerel and pollack.

Overnight Line.   Leaving a line out at night (fig. 99) may be the lazy man's way, but there is nothing like having the line work for you while you are asleep. Stretch the line out between two trees or boulders or just anchor it with pegs. Hang as many traces from it as you like. Floats can be made from small pieces of driftwood. Allow for the movement of the tide so that any fish caught are not left high and dry during the night.

Jigging.   The paternoster trace is ideal for jigging up and down (fig. 100). This is an excellent method of catching many different types of fish, especially mackerel. About six traces can be fastened to one line. Any more than this and the whole setup becomes downright dangerous if you fill all the hooks at the same time, which is not difficult when the mackerel are running. Feathers or plastic eels can be used as a lure, and the line is moved slowly up and down while the kayak is stationary.

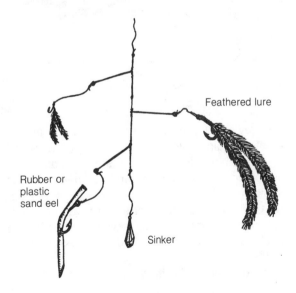

Feathered lure

Rubber or plastic sand eel

Sinker

100. The paternoster trace.

Gaffing.   If the area you visit has an abundance of salmon streams, you may find that gaffing is

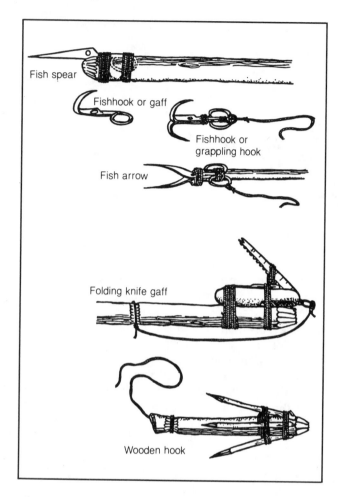

Fish spear

Fishhook or gaff

Fishhook or grappling hook

Fish arrow

Folding knife gaff

Wooden hook

101. Fishing implements made from scissors, a folding knife, or wood.

an easy way to fill your cooking pot. You can improvise a gaff by using scissors, a folding knife, or wood (see fig. 101). Next, find a salmon stream. Look for a shallow place, either at the mouth or below rapids and hook the salmon out as they fight their way upstream. Gaffing is not the sportsman's way of catching salmon, but that is hardly a valid consideration when your stomach is empty. You can always apologize to the salmon as it is baking in foil!

A word of warning: if, when you arrive at your chosen fishing spot, there are a lot of half-chewed salmon lying about and you are in bear country, be on your guard or go somewhere else.

Making Nets and Hooks.   Small hand-fishing nets can be made from string vests or mosquito netting. Fishhooks can be adapted from old fish bones, safety pins, or sail needles softened in a fire and bent to shape.

Gathering Food from the Shoreline

If you do not have much luck with your rod and line skills, do not give up. There are other ways of gaining sustenance from the sea—just go out and pick it up. The old Aleut saying, "When the tide is out the table is set," is as true now as it ever was. Having lived all my life by the seacoast, I grew up with children who ate whelks, mussels, and crabs the way others eat candy. Precautions must be taken however, because most rock seafoods must be properly collected and prepared and eaten fresh. In most cases, the creatures are cooked while still alive.

One strong word of warning: before kayaking in an area where you intend to eat inshore seafood, inquire to make sure that pollution from mercury or a red tide has not rendered the animals highly dangerous for human consumption.

Limpets.   Limpets (fig. 102A) can be found on almost any seashore on rocks at low tide. The secret is to quickly pull them off the rocks before they have time to get a good grip.

The keyhole limpet (fig. 102B) is not a true limpet, but it looks like one because of its coolie hat shape and the muscular foot on the bottom. It is just as good to eat as a limpet, and it can be identified by the missing apex of the shell leaving an almost round hole. The shell is usually gray in color or has brown and white radiating ridges.

To prepare limpets, loosen them from the shell with a knife and cut off the foot portion. Limpets are tough, so put them between some muslin cloth and beat them with a piece of wood—or a meat mallet if you have one—to tenderize them. Limpets can be boiled or panfried alone or with batter. If you carry a portable mincer, you can mince the limpets to use in a chowder or to give body to a soup.

Whelks.   Whelks (fig. 102C and D) are sea snails. They come in any number of varieties and are eaten throughout the world. They also come in a variety of colors and shapes. Some shells are smooth and some are wrinkled, and they vary in size from one to two inches. The opening at the bottom is closed by a hard trapdoor, which is attached to the edible foot of the animal.

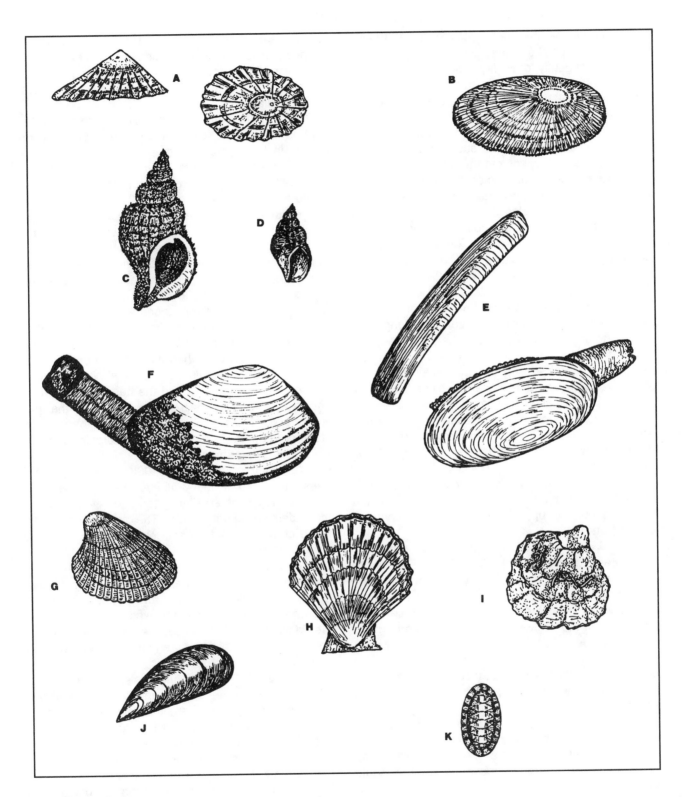

102. Edible shellfish.

To prepare, let the whelks soak for about three to four hours. Scrub the shells, cover them with water, and boil them gently for twenty minutes. Drain the water off and chill them. A pin will help you remove the snail from it shell. When you do this, the intestines will stay in the shell, so you can eat all you pull out. They can be dipped in melted butter or in a cocktail or tartar sauce if you have had room for such luxuries. You can also grind them up as you did the limpets.

Clams. The soft bodies of clams (fig. 102E and F) are enclosed, or partially so, by two shells, which can be tightly closed. The body of the razor clam is not completely enclosed by its smooth, brown, shiny shell. They are good to eat, but you will have to be fast to catch them because they can bury and hide themselves under the sand very quickly.

To prepare razor clams, place them in containers filled with salt water and allow them to clean themselves for several hours. Then run a sharp knife along each side of the shell to cut the muscle that holds the shell shut and allows it to open. If you intend to fry the whole clam, use a pair of scissors to cut through the next siphon. The dark-colored stuff near the hinge is the liver, which is nutritious and full of flavor.

The littleneck clam is also called the rock or butter clam and varies in color from gray or cream to a mottled brown or yellow. Shells grow to about two inches across.

To prepare littleneck clams, wash with a brush before steaming in a small amount of water. Once the shell has opened up, the clam may be served in melted butter.

Cockles. When looked at from the side, cockles appear heart-shaped (fig. 102G). They are to be found just under the surface in sand or mud.

To prepare cockles, leave them for several hours in a bucket of seawater in the shade so that they have time to clean themselves of all their mud and grit.

Scallops. Scallops (fig. 102H) are easily recognized by their fan-shaped shells, which seem to be collected all over the world. Most scallops swim by opening and shutting their shells. They are found in shallow water.

To prepare scallops, slide a sharp knife between the shells and cut the holding muscle. The shells will then come apart easily. Cover the animal with bread crumbs and fry, or wrap in bacon and broil, or sauté in butter.

Oysters. Oysters (fig. 102I) have irregular-shaped shells, which are fluted in gray and white. They vary in shape, depending on the particular species—some tend to be elongated while others are more circular.

To prepare oysters, cut the hinge muscle as described for clams. Oysters can be eaten raw or dipped in batter made from a mixture of eggs and milk. They can then be rolled in whole wheat flour or cornmeal and fried for a couple of minutes in hot fat or oil.

Mussels. Mussels (fig. 102J) are found all over the world—I know because I always seem to be scratching my kayak on mussel beds! The shells are blue, black, or brown and grow in colonies on just about any solid object. When cooked, the animals turn an orange-brown. To reduce the risk of eating polluted mussels, eat only those that are exposed to the air for long periods of time. Be sure to inquire about the area in which you are gathering them. The livers of mussels collect harmful nitrates from the sea.

To prepare mussels, scrape the shells to remove the seaweed, barnacles, and the beards (sometimes known as "dead man's hair"—but don't let that put you off). Wash them thoroughly and put them into a steamer to open, then eat them after dipping them in hot butter or lemon sauce.

Chitons. Chitons (fig. 102K) are strange creatures that are to be found all over the world near the low tide mark. The smaller ones attach themselves to the undersides of small rocks. The giant chiton can be found crawling about on seaweed or rocks, near the low tide mark.

To prepare chitons, be sure to clean them immediately after they are gathered because they deteriorate rapidly. Pull the smooth foot off from the underneath, then scrape and wash. The Indians of the Pacific Coast used to eat them raw. If you prefer, chitons can be beaten into tenderness and fried with egg batter or crisp crumbs.

Octopus. You might find a small octopus (fig. 103) stranded by the tide or hiding in the crevices of a rocky pool. They live on small crustaceans and mollusks, so do not worry about finding the remains of one of the local divers in its stomach.

To prepare octopus, first remove the skin. This can be done by rubbing with a coarse salt. Keep rinsing well with water and continue rubbing until the skin can tear off easily. The arms can be cut into thin slices and smoked, or the meat can be pounded until tender and fried in bread crumbs. Do not overfry octopus or it will get tough.

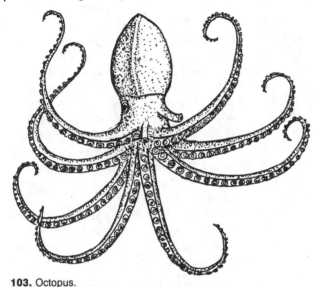

103. Octopus.

104. Giant red sea urchin.

Sea Urchins.   I once had three or four very large, spiny sea urchins (fig. 104) busily wandering and crackling about underneath my spray cover in the cockpit area of my kayak. It was at the end of a hot summer day and I was wearing a pair of swimming trunks and a T-shirt. I forgot all about them until I decided to treat myself to an Eskimo roll to cool off. It was only when I had my head upside down in the water that I was reminded that I was not alone in the cockpit. I probably executed the fastest roll on record. Earlier that day, I watched in horror while one of the lighthouse keepers on Northumberland's Longstone Lighthouse picked up one of my urchins. He proceeded to stick his fingers inside, scoop out the eggs, and eat them raw. He assured me afterwards that these were a great delicacy. In a kayak, it is an easy matter to collect sea urchins. You will see them clinging to rocks just below the surface as you paddle along. Kill them only if you are going to eat them. It is surely wrong to kill a living creature just because it is beautiful or interesting to look at.

To prepare sea urchins, you can boil them in their shells and then split open the shells to obtain the meat. Many people, like the lighthouse keeper, consider the eggs a delicacy. If you wish, however,

the eggs can be washed out with the rest of the internal organs. In Australia, live sea urchins are thrown into an open fire to burn off the spines. The shells are then opened and the insides eaten while still hot.

Barnacles.   Barnacles (fig. 105) are to be found all over the world, and all the types are edible. The gooseneck barnacle is usually found in rocky crevices in areas where there is big surf. Ships also have barnacles, and you might even prize one from the back of a friendly whale.

To prepare barnacles, cook them as soon as possible after collection. Wash carefully in fresh water, then put a little water in the bottom of a steamer pan. As soon as the water starts to boil, put the barnacles in the top of the pan. When they can be handled, remove the top part and the rough skin. The meat is red and resembles that of a crab, but it has more flavor.

105. Barnacles.

Shrimp.   You will find shrimp (fig. 106) in rock pools at low tide. To prepare, drop them into a pan of boiling salted water and let them boil for fifteen to twenty minutes. Then pour off the hot water and cool them in cold water. Hold the body tightly, then break off the head and peel away the thin shell. The shrimp can then be eaten as part of a salad or fried in batter.

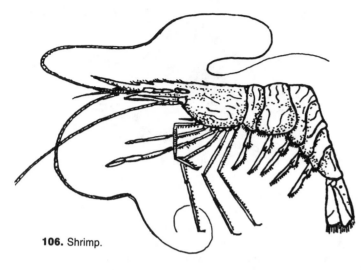

106. Shrimp.

Crabs and Lobsters. Because crabs and lobsters are more common than some of the other sea creatures I have discussed, I will not go into detail about how to catch them. Traps are usually required, though you may be fortunate enough to find them in tide pools or shallow water. Crabs and lobsters should be dropped live into boiling salted water and cooked for twenty minutes.

Some Simple Ropework

If you happen to be a climber as well as a kayaker—and many people seem to be able to combine these activities quite well—then by all means carry the special equipment with you inside your boat. The advice I give here is for the nonclimber who just happens to find himself in an awkward position, but who has had the presence of mind to carry a length of rope as part of his equipment.

Finding yourself stormbound on some tiny beach is not so rare as you may think. If the beach is on a headland or promontory, there may be calm water quite close at hand, but you are separated from it by steep rocks and cliffs. This will mean a strenuous portage. A knowledge of simple ropework may save injury to yourself and prevent your equipment from bouncing down a cliff. Knowing how to lower yourself and your kayak is also important. On the other hand, if you take part in some careless glacier walking, you could finish up down a crevasse and if you cannot climb a rope, you might not get out again.

Abseiling. Lowering yourself down a cliff on a rope is not so difficult if you know how. In the method known as the classic abseil or rappel (fig. 107) the rope is doubled around an anchor or belay point, so that both halves of the rope hang down.

To perform this maneuver, walk slowly backward down the slope or face, keeping your legs at right angles to it if possible. The speed of your descent is adjusted by the angle of the rope held in the right hand. The rope should be held firmly but not tightly in the left hand. With the rope around your right thigh and left shoulder, lean back and let the strain be taken on those areas. The right leg should be kept lower than the left, with the rope well up under your behind. Remember to lower yourself slowly to avoid bad friction burns that could make paddling your kayak very uncomfortable.

Long descents by this method can be very painful, but it is ideal for drops of fifteen to twenty feet or for slowly keeping pace with a kayak, which is also making its way down a cliff.

107. The classic abseil is a good method of lowering yourself down a cliff.

Lowering a Kayak. In figure 108, the man could quite easily make a couple of turns around the tree with the rope and lower the kayak in that fashion. If the ledge is narrow, the paddler must belay (secure)

108. Lowering a kayak down a cliff.

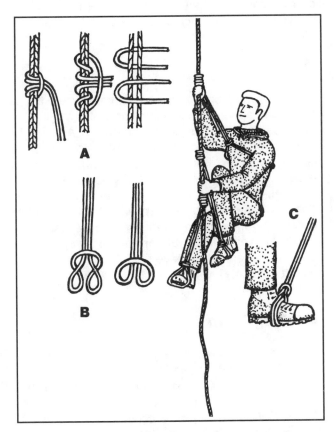

109. Climbing a rope with the use of a Prusik knot.

himself around a rock or to a peg hammered into the rock.

Climbing a Rope.   No matter how strong you are, if you are frightened, the rope is thin, and your hands are cold, you are certainly not going to climb it. Unfortunately, you may have fallen into a crevasse, and you cannot stay there forever.

You will need three separated loops of rope dropped down to you. These can be taken from the towlines of the kayaks, but make sure that the loops are thinner than the rope you intend to climb. Your ascent is made possible by what is known as a Prusik knot (fig. 109). This knot can be pushed up or along a rope quite easily when there is no tension on the loop; but the moment any sudden pressure is put on it, the loop will grip fast to the main rope (fig. 109A and B).

This method of climbing with Prusik knots takes some practice, but is easily mastered (fig. 109C). First take the weight off one foot and slide up the knot on that side as high as it will go. Then put your weight back on the higher foot, take it off the lower foot, and slide the lower knot as high as it will go. Next take the weight of your body on both feet and slide up the knot from the chest rope as high as you can. Continue in this manner until the rope is climbed. This is a slow method of gaining height, but it is reliable and foolproof so long as the rope and anchor point are strong.

Glaciers

Many glaciers eventually find their way to the sea, and to paddle near to them is an unforgettable experience. As you paddle closer to the base of a glacier, the danger increases. At any time huge quantities of ice can fall from the face with a thunderous roar, creating quite alarming tidal waves.

Glacial ice exhibits the most beautiful shades of blues and greens and the temptation to wander across this turquoise wonderland is a real one.

If you feel that a glacier might lie on your route, you are well advised to carry certain items of equipment: at least one length of good climbing rope, an ice ax, and a pair of crampons for each person.

Crampons.   Crampons are strapped to your boots to prevent you from slipping on ice. They have ten or twelve sharp points that bite into the snow or ice and enable you to walk safely. The twelve-pointed crampons are probably the best to use because they have two forward points that can be kicked straight into a steep ice slope. Crampons must fit the boots tightly. Slack crampons will feel insecure and are dangerous, especially when walking sideways (traversing) across a slope. When you are traversing, place your feet flat to the ice slope. Make sure that all the points are in contact with the ice face. Keep the crampon points protected when not in use.

Ice Ax.   The best ice ax for general use is the traditional type with the long shaft. When held by the head, the shaft should be long enough for the end to touch the ground (making the ice ax ideal for using as a walking stick). Ice axes have a wide adze blade on one side of the head for cutting steps in snow and, on the other side, a sharp spike for cutting into hard ice. At the end of the ax there is a pointed ferrule, handy to use as a probe to test the depth of the snow. All ice axes should be fitted with a sling.

When walking on ice, hold the ice ax like a walking stick, with the sling around your wrist and the adze toward you. If you hold the ax like this, getting into the correct position to stop a slide will be almost automatic. The second you feel yourself falling, roll onto your front and force the point into the snow, the head of the ax level with your shoulder (fig. 110A). The shaft should slope down across your body to the opposite side. Hold the shaft three-quarters of the way down with the left hand. To help dig the point in deep, lever from the elbow.

Do not stick the point into the ice too hard or too suddenly. Otherwise the ax might be snatched out of your hand. As you slide, try to exert an even pressure. On very steep slopes, the friction can be increased by lifting your body clear at the thighs so your knees press into the snow (fig. 110B). If you are wearing crampons, you must keep them clear of the face in this manner because they can dig in and cause you to somersault and lose control. This happened to one of my friends and he was skewered through the ribs on his own ice ax. Luckily, he survived.

Snow Hole

I can remember a number of unfortunate things that have happened to tents on some of my trips. One tent was half-eaten by pack rats on the Aleutian Islands, another was completely burnt out on a Scottish island. If your tent is lost or destroyed, and the ground is deep with snow, there is certainly no need to freeze to death—just build a snow hole or a snowhouse. There are two points to remember, however. First, construct your sleeping area well above floor level (fig. 111)—you will be warmer the higher up you are. Second, remember to leave a ventilation hole so you do not suffocate.

Getting Help

There are numerous ways to signal for assistance.
- Fire a gun at intervals of one minute—but do not blast off all your ammunition if you think there is no one to hear.
- Sound your fog horn continually.
- Set off any red flare, parachute flare, dyemarker, or orange smoke.

110. The ice ax self-arrest.

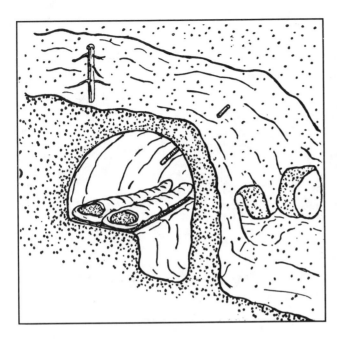

111. If your tent is lost or destroyed, you can build a shelter in the snow.

- Spell out SOS in sand or snow or flash Morse code with a torch or mirror.
- Repeat ''mayday'' on a radio telephone.
- Activate a radio beacon.
- Slowly raise and lower your arms.
- Wave a paddle slowly from side to side above your head.
- Send someone paddling off to get help.
- Set three fires in a triangle—this is accepted by pilots as a distress signal.
- Blow blasts on a whistle in groups of six.
- Make a smoky fire with leaves or rags.
- Fly a parafoil kite above tree level. They are easy to see and could also carry up a radio antenna.

Signaling with Mirrors.   Signaling with mirrors is one of the most effective ways of attracting attention, so it is well worth making an effort to master the skills involved. The reflection of sunlight in a small mirror can be seen for many miles and so would be readily seen by a potential rescuer if he is looking your way, and if you can aim the direction of the mirror flash. While the former is up to providence, you can definitely do something about the latter.

To make sure your flashes get somewhere near the target, you need a special two-sided mirror with a

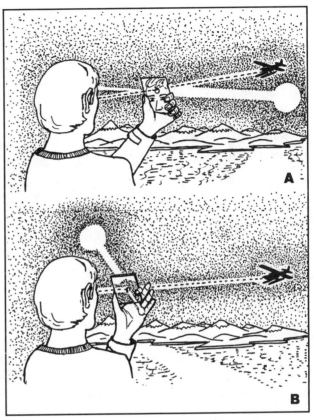

112. Signaling with mirrors is an effective way of attracting attention.

small hole in the middle. These signaling mirrors can be obtained at outdoor equipment stores or surplus stores. To signal your rescuer, first hold the mirror at arm's length and sight the plane (or whatever) through the small hole. If the plane is somewhere near the same position as the sun, move the mirrored side which faces you until you can see the sunlight spot coming through the hole and shining on your face. Keep moving the mirror until this spot of sunlight coincides with the hole in the center. The spot will appear to vanish into the hole in the center and, if the plane is still in the center of this hole, it will get a flashing reflection from your mirror (fig. 112A).

The sun, unfortunately, may not be near the object of our signaling. If the sun is well to the side and is more than a right angle from the target, hold the mirror so that it shines through the center hole and falls on the palm of your hand (fig. 112B). Line up this little circle of brightness as seen in the mirror so that its

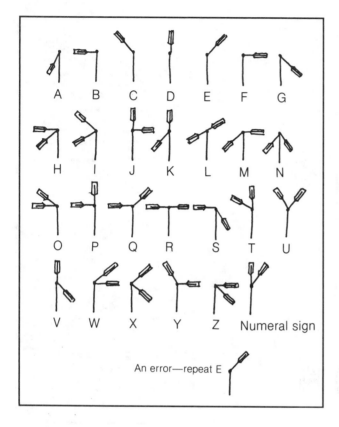

An error—repeat E

113. Semaphore.

· —	Alpha	— ·	November

Alpha ·—   November —·
Bravo —···   Oscar ———
Charlie —·—·   Papa ·——·
Delta —··   Quebec ——·—
Echo ·   Romeo ·—·
Foxtrot ··—·   Sierra ···
Golf ——·   Tango —
Hotel ····   Uniform ··—
Item ··   Victor ···—
Juliet ·———   Whiskey ·——
Kilo —·—   X-ray —··—
Lima ·—··   Yankee —·——
Mike ——   Zulu ——··

November —·
Oscar ———
Papa ·——·
Quebec ——·—
Romeo ·—·
Sierra ···
Tango —
Uniform ··—
Victor ···—
Whiskey ·——
X-ray —··—
Yankee —·——
Zulu ——··

114. Morse code with phonetic alphabet.

Morse Code and Semaphore. I certainly do not expect the kayak paddlers who read this book to rush immediately to learn by heart either the Morse code or the system of relaying messages by semaphore (fig. 113). However, there may be a number of occasions when both could be very useful; perhaps a group becomes separated but are within sight of one another across the stormy waters between two islands. It would certainly be quite easy to pass messages by semaphore.

I would suggest, therefore, that both the Morse code and semaphore be inscribed or scratched somewhere—for instance on the inside of a hatch cover.

reflection vanishes through the center hole of the mirror in the same way as when the sun fell on your face.

If this all sounds too complicated, and well it might, there is a simpler way although it is not as accurate. Hold your thumb up at arm's length. Sight your thumb under the target and flash the sun's reflection along your arm and off your thumb up onto the target. Try this first on a nearby tree or rock.

PLANNING A TRIP

A journey can be planned as much as a year ahead of time with the help of tide tables, charts, and a *Tidal Stream Atlas.* However, the prevailing conditions determine whether the trip will go ahead as planned.

It is incumbent on paddlers to acquaint themselves with local meteorological conditions that might cause sudden changes in the weather. It is also important to be able to interpret any weather information that appears in the press or on the radio and television. The possession of a small radio permanently tuned to continuous weather forecasts can be a priceless piece of equipment.

The most accurate weather forecasts are good only up to six hours or so. The immediate difference that an increase in wind strength or a change in the direction of the tide can make must always be foremost in one's mind.

The factor that governs the length of the trip and the degree of commitment possible is the strength and ability of the weakest member of the group.

At best the group will travel only at the speed of the slowest member. If the weather turns foul, a situation could occur that might easily get out of hand. Having to rescue inexperienced kayakers or having to tow them to safety places enormous burdens on the more experienced members of a party.

It is vital to know the coastline involved and apart from the necessary navigation and seamanship, it is also important to have an understanding of the subjects contained in this book. Remember that paddlers have been known to become very sick in their kayaks, to become affected by the sun's glare off the water, to become overheated, hypothermic, and to be taken ill. Never, therefore, undertake more than a simple journey with good escape routes in the company of untried, inexperienced paddlers who are unknown to you.

The average rate at which a small party of competent but inexperienced paddlers will travel is probably two knots plus the speed of the tidal stream. A strong head wind could drop this to one knot or less overall, and thus throw off your estimated time of arrival (ETA) and subsequent estimated time of departure (ETD). You, must, therefore, appoint someone of sound judgment and someone who has an appreciation of the factors affecting sea journeys to remain on shore and serve as an emergency contact. If the need arises, this person can alert rescue services and save valuable time that the authorities might spend wondering whether or not you are really in trouble.

Preparing for Short Trips

If you are about to lead a group of eager kayakers on a sea trip—even a short one—the following checklist should run through your mind. Taking extra time at the beginning of a journey may save you a great deal of heartache later on. Take time to consider the following questions:

- Am I going far enough to merit informing the

Coast Guard? If so, I will tell them: my name and qualifications; how many there are in the group; the type and color of our kayaks; what distress signals we carry; where we are going, the time we expect to return, and any other relevant details.

- Are all the kayaks and spray covers serviceable and in good repair—no loose toggles or footrests?
- Are the boats full of flotation that will remain in them in the event of a capsize?
- Are the kits carried on the kayak decks fastened on tight?
- Who is carrying flares?
- Is everyone dressed adequately?
- Who looks the weakest?
- Does anyone have a special disability (such as deafness or diabetes)?
- Am I taking them too far?
- Do I have enough help for what I intend to do with the group?
- Did I get a weather forecast?
- Have I taken the tides into consideration?
- Have I got all my own equipment?
- Did I lock the car?

During your deliberations, you may consider that one person in the group could put you all at risk. This might be due to the distance involved, the condition of the sea and weather, the state of his equipment, or some physical or psychological problems. If this is the case, he must be left behind. Be particularly careful in the case of someone who has been recommended to you by someone else. Do not let feeling sorry for him or the persuasion of others deter you from a decision you feel is right and has the best interest of the group at heart.

When launching, involve your group in a study of the sequence and patterns of the oncoming waves so that they will become familiar with the driest and most efficient way of getting out through surf. Impress upon them the importance of keeping dry during extended expeditions that involve camping.

If the surf is dumping, the leader must leave the beach last. Launch the group one at a time. Hold each paddler steady at the water's edge so the wave will not sweep his boat sideways. As soon as there is a lull in the oncoming waves, push the boat off and out to sea. An outflowing rip will help considerably to get everyone clear of the beach.

Leading a Group

There should be no doubt about who the leader is. On the open sea, the ratio of leaders to students should be not fewer than one to eight. The leader should appoint a pathfinder to paddle out in front. If the conditions ahead are questionable or the route is uncertain, then the leader should go to the front. Under normal conditions, however, the leader will move about among the group offering advice and encouragement should anyone need it. Train your group to be aware of one another; show them how to twist their bodies around and turn their heads by trailing the back of their paddle blade on the water, thus looking right around on that side.

Members of a group should not paddle too far from one another. In rough seas and big swells, individuals can be hidden in the troughs. Some audible or visual signals such as a fog horn or a whistle should be agreed upon before the trip.

During rock-dodging or game-playing exercises close inshore, leaders should be careful not to let the members of their groups get behind rocks or into caves where they can be out of sight for more than a few minutes.

Do not take untried novices into situations where they have to cope with steep following seas a long way offshore until they have done simple forward-running exercises close to the beach.

Landing. If you approach a beach where the surf is much larger than your group is used to, or, if the surf is dumping dangerously, stop well outside the surf line and explain to everyone what you intend to do and what you intend they should do to get ashore safely. Instruct the group to paddle in one at a time; then, if there is a capsize, you will only have one casualty to worry about. As they paddle in to shore, they must keep turning around and watching for any large waves approaching from behind. As soon as a wave reaches them, and if it is steep, the student should stop paddling or even back paddle if the wave is very large to prevent the kayak from surging forward and going out of control at surf speed. Once they have allowed the wave to pass under them, they must paddle fast again until the next wave catches up to them. As the paddlers reach shallow water where the waves are breaking, they must pause and wait for a lull in the big wave sets and then paddle in on the backs of smaller waves. Appoint someone to take charge and keep an eye on things while you go ashore first and land. The individuals can then be guided in one at a time with the help of some prearranged signals such as "Take care, wave behind," "Slow down," "Paddle fast." Once a boat reaches the beach, grab the toggle quickly and pull the man to safety.

Coping with Incidents. When a boat needs repair or there is a capsize, everyone should face the oncoming waves and hold their position close to the action without knocking into one another or impeding those involved in sorting out the problem. There will be a tendency for someone to start paddling off, and the rest will follow. It is vital that the leader keep this from happening. Therefore, it is better that the leader is not committed to the rescue, repair, tow, or whatever it may be. There could be times when speed is of the essence, however, and this is when the leader must deal with the matter at hand while at the same time keeping a watchful eye on the rest of the group.

Rafting up the rest of the party in this situation is not a desirable practice. (A raft is formed when two or more paddlers bring their kayaks alongside and connect them together by placing their paddles across the foredecks and holding on to each other's boat.) The raft drifts more quickly than an individual kayak and much more quickly than someone in the water holding on to a boat. It is extremely difficult for the raft to be maintained in waves, and when it comes to splitting up and proceeding with the trip, there could be considerable danger of capsize.

If a situation gets so out of hand that help is needed and certain individual paddlers are in danger of capsizing, rafting up in pairs is a good way of containing matters until help arrives. If, however, it is obvious that everyone might finish up by being blown out to sea, it is better for the group to maintain a course that keeps them paddling into the waves with the kayaks angled slightly into the wind. By angling into the wind, the boats are pointing into the waves and are less likely to capsize. It is hoped that the group can get itself close enough to the shore for the situation to be resolved.

The different effects of tide and wind should be noted. When the wind is against the tide, paddled kayaks or kayaks floating empty and high on the surface are more affected by the wind unless the tidal stream is very strong and the wind very light. Anyone in the water or a waterlogged kayak will move in the direction of the tidal stream, regardless of the strength of the wind. When the wind is blowing across the tidal stream, anyone in the water or a waterlogged boat will move in the direction of the tide with some pull by wind and wave action.

Planning an Expedition

Today there are not many corners of the globe left unexplored—perhaps "unspoiled" would be a better word. The kayak has certain highly specialized qualities, and it is the unique features of this craft that enable us to rediscover the world in which we live. Even familiar and well-trodden coastlines are giving up secrets to the inquisitive paddler. Expeditions led by kayak, therefore, may be to areas where others have been before, but the paddler is permitted to view the coastline from a different angle.

From a kayak one does truly see the world from a different angle. I remember gazing up at some sea cliffs in Baja California. There was a strata of volcanic ash that held the contents of some prehistoric seabed. The multitude of shells within this layer were still intact, the pressures of time had not yet turned these mollusks into fossils. It was as if I were watching history in the making. I felt a little smug as I thought that no craft other than a kayak would have been able to get close enough to shore to see this phenomenon, and that it would have been completely invisible to anyone walking along the top of the cliff.

It is sometimes difficult to decide which aspect of an expedition gives the most satisfaction—the actual paddling or the planning and preparations that take place during the months (sometimes years) beforehand. A tremendous amount of preparation goes into a comparatively small expedition, so allow at least one year to prepare any expedition in a foreign country. This preparatory stage is known as doing your homework, and for a start it means reading every book you can lay your hands on that contains information on the area you intend to visit. It is often a good idea to delegate certain areas of preparatory study to different members of the group. You will need to know all there is to know about the local weather, the people, the coastline, the topography of the area, what you can eat, and what will eat you. If your research leads you to believe that the locals do not speak English, it might be worthwhile either to write down or learn a few phrases that might come in handy.

Letters will have to be written for advice, and it is certainly no good being proud. The best people to contact are explorers, scientists, mountaineers, or kayakers who have been to the area you intend to visit or one with similar conditions. Local information can be had from the local airlines or bush pilots, Coast Guard, or similar organization, and the public information service in the foreign embassy of the country you intend to visit. If you make a bona fide inquiry you will find the armed forces quite forthcoming with information.

Promoting the Expedition. If you expect to ask for sponsorship from firms or individuals, you should send them an outline of your proposed expedition and a personal letter. The outline of your expedition should include:

- The inclusive dates.
- A list of the members and their qualifications, their functions on the expedition, and any previous experience.
- The locality, with a map and insets to show specific locations.
- A brief outline of your aims and objectives (whether photographic, scientific, sporting, competitive).
- A background to the proposed expedition.
- Your plans versus what others have done in the past.
- The names of any supporting or sponsoring scientific bodies.
- Your plans for any specimens you bring back.
- How you will reward individual sponsors (either by publishing photographs of you using their product or including their name on photographs used by others).

You must satisfy the needs of sponsors so that any expeditions following in your footsteps will not be rebuffed when they apply for assistance.

Calculating Costs. You must be realistic and up-to-date with your expenses. There will be the cost of duplicating and postage so that your handout can be distributed. Air fares, overland transport, hire of vehicles or charter planes must be considered. In some parts of the world it may be necessary to hire porters. The price of fuel and consequently the cost of some kinds of transportation vary greatly in different parts of the world. Insurance will be necessary for yourselves and the kayaks. The kayaks may also

have to be packaged and stored. You may have to subsist in civilization or while waiting for any unexpected contingencies (weather, repairs, or boats delayed by customs).

The type of food to be carried must be decided upon (dehydrated or freeze-dried). Is it to be ordered abroad and delivered to your launching base or is it to be transported from the expedition's country of origin? Special equipment to be considered includes distress radios or beacons, cameras and film, medical supplies, firearms and ammunition. Finally, the cost of publishing an expedition report at the end of the trip has to be considered.

Choosing Companions. Choosing the right people for a kayak expedition into wilderness areas can be crucial to the success of your venture. Constraints of time and money may force incompatible paddlers together. It often comes as a shock when paddlers with a common interest in sea kayaking find they have nothing else in common. Long-standing friends may become unrecognizable when confronted with the stress of an arduous trip or the challenges of a hostile environment.

Personality clashes can mean the failure of an expedition. It is essential, therefore, to assess each member of your expedition as thoroughly as possible. Probably the best way to do this is to spend as much time as possible paddling together before the trip.

Coping with Dissension. In a wilderness situation, the battle against fatigue, anxiety, and the elements can be very one-sided, particularly when loneliness has to be faced as a result of character clashes, dissension, petty recriminations, and jealousies generated in small groups formed among expedition members.

Although cliques are obviously undesirable in any situation, they are more easily absorbed—and may sometimes even go unnoticed—if the expedition is a large one. With small kayak expeditions, however, cliques or minority factions can jeopardize the success of the whole venture.

In a survival situation demoralization makes individuals easy prey to exposure. Any clique which excludes a minority can cause the smaller group to fight for survival in no uncertain terms. Loneliness can do strange things: it either brings individuals to the verge of collapse, or it forces them to withdraw into themselves for protection and comfort. It is while drawing upon that

115. Baidarka Explorer ready to be loaded with a month's supply of equipment. (Photo by the author.)

inner strength while the chance of survival is slipping out of his own hands, that a man will place himself in the hands of God.

Loneliness, anxiety, doubt, fear, despair, and apprehension are all nails in the coffin of survival, and in this kind of situation, one's companions can be a deciding factor in the battle to survive. A man who has trustworthy men and true friends by his side can overcome fear; even death can be faced with calmness and fortitude if the comfort that friendship can bring is at hand.

Importance of a Leader. Before considering what qualities a leader should possess, we might question why there should be a leader at all. First it is important that there is one individual who can act and speak for the expedition as a whole because with special status this person will be more able to negotiate with such people as customs agents or foreign embassies. If your expedition is one of special merit,

it may be necessary to meet and bargain with film or television companies, and once again it is better to leave negotiations to one person. A well-known and respected person who is designated leader can give credulity to a scheme that at first glance might seem impossible to the uninitiated public. Sponsors are happier if they know that someone is responsible for fulfilling the expedition's promises of photographs and publicity articles that show their products in an interesting or exciting manner.

Someone must also be able to take the responsibility if or when things start to go wrong; these can range from missing items of equipment to serious injury or loss of life.

It would be ridiculous for any one person to try to do all the organizing jobs himself. For that reason, the leader will have to spread the load and delegate some of the jobs. By knowing his group well, the leader is in the best position to allocate tasks to those members of the group who are best suited to undertake them. In this way jobs will not be duplicated during the more hectic stages of preparation.

Good leaders should be diplomatic, and all major problems should be discussed by the whole group, although the final decision should be with the person who take the overall responsibility. Regardless of personality, there must be something about the leader that inspires others to place their confidence and trust in him.

No matter how democratic the discussions have been in planning, preparation, and initial stages of the expedition, inevitably there will be a time when a decision must be made with no time for discussion or debate. At such a time the leader must feel able to make this decision and others must have sufficient trust to abide by it.

Because the decisions of the leader could affect the lives of every member of the expedition, the person who leads must be the master of his own craft in the broadest sense of the word, whether it be rock-climbing, skiing, or kayaking. This does not necessarily mean that the leader should be the strongest or the most skillful. However, his competence and vast experience should inspire confidence in any decision he makes, especially with regard to the navigational and safety aspects of the expedition.

The leader should be sensitive to any problems or discomfort suffered by the group as a whole or any individual member who has a specific physical or psychological problem during the trip or even during the preparatory stages before the expedition sets off.

A good leader should be farsighted enough to anticipate problems before they occur. For example, in cases of friction between members of the group, the leader should act as a calming influence and serve as a mediator.

Because the alternative to crying is often laughing, expedition leaders would be well advised to cultivate their sense of humor. Many an expedition has been held together by a good laugh when everything seems to have gone miserably wrong.

Far-Reaching Responsibilities

As an ocean kayaker you can be considered more than just a sportsman once you become competent. With advanced skills and good equipment, you are a highly trained operative who has the facility to offer help and relief to many people in different ways.

Your kayak can assist in rescues impossible for other craft because it can pick its way through drifting ice or floating logs. Its shallow draft also allows it to navigate close inshore over kelp beds where no other vessel would be able to go.

The distress flares that you have with you can be sent skyward on behalf of others, while the compass on your deck could help guide less prudent water users who are lost in thick fog.

You should be carrying a small but well-stocked first aid kit. Then it would not be difficult for you to leave your kayak and board another small vessel to administer assistance should this become necessary.

Your repair kit can also be used on behalf of others. My pliers have cut fishhooks from the fingers of careless fishermen, and the repair tape has been used to bind up leaking fuel pipes. The life jacket or buoyancy aid you wear can be taken off and given to someone in greater need, perhaps someone already in distress in the water. If a small boat were to sink completely, quite a number of people could hang on around your gunwale and be supported. This would have to be done evenly around the boat so that your stability would be maintained.

High winds do not blow kindly on small motorboats with engine failure, but a strong paddler can usually hold a small boat and prevent it from drifting onto rocks by using his towline.

Using the buoyancy of a kayak as support, assistance can be given to anyone trapped by extensive mud flats or quicksand.

To sum up, the presence of a calm, experienced, and well-equipped man in a craft as versatile and as seaworthy as today's ocean kayak should be a source of reassurance and an asset to all other water users.

Conclusion

I have tried in some way to prepare you for quite a few of the problems that may arise both on and off the water. I have no doubt, however, that on your travels you will make some brand new mistakes and encounter some brand new problems all your own—some perhaps of your own making. And like me, you will probably paddle the wrong boat in the wrong weather in the wrong place and with badly chosen companions. And like those who have paddled before you, you will learn by your mistakes, but whether you fight against screaming winds or glide serenely across a velvet carpet of early morning mist, revel in the mastery of your craft and enjoy every second.

So take your beautiful replica of the hunter's boat and rediscover the world—or perhaps just rediscover your world—in the sunshine and in the company of true friends. The ocean is all yours.

It is calm, the smooth sea heaves in a long
swell towards the rocky islets that fringe the
shore, a light haze still lies over the sounds
between them, and the sea-birds floating on the
surface seem double their natural size. The
kaiaks cut their way forwards, side by side,
making only a silent ripple; the paddles swing
in an even rhythm, while the men keep up an
unbroken stream of conversation, and now and
then burst out into merry laughter. (Nansen,
Eskimo Life, pp. 59–60.)

INDEX